Praise for *Retail Superstars*

"Far beyond price and product . . . it's all about the 'sizzle' that independent retailers give customers. No need to invent a successful wheel . . . just add your own unique spokes to any of these twenty-five and you'll be on the road to making your store a superstar."

—William H. Baxter, former president/CEO,
Retail Merchants Association

Retail Superstars

Retail Superstars

Inside the **25 Best** Independent Stores in America

GEORGE WHALIN

PORTFOLIO

PORTFOLIO

Published by the Penguin Group • Penguin Group (USA) Inc., 375 Hudson Street, New York, New York 10014, U.S.A. • Penguin Group (Canada), 90 Eglinton Avenue East, Suite 700, Toronto, Ontario, Canada M4P 2Y3 (a division of Pearson Penguin Canada Inc.) • Penguin Books Ltd, 80 Strand, London WC2R 0RL, England • Penguin Ireland, 25 St. Stephen's Green, Dublin 2, Ireland (a division of Penguin Books Ltd) • Penguin Books Australia Ltd, 250 Camberwell Road, Camberwell, Victoria 3124, Australia (a division of Pearson Australia Group Pty Ltd) • Penguin Books India Pvt Ltd, 11 Community Centre, Panchsheel Park, New Delhi – 110 017, India • Penguin Group (NZ), 67 Apollo Drive, Rosedale, North Shore 0632, New Zealand (a division of Pearson New Zealand Ltd) • Penguin Books (South Africa) (Pty) Ltd, 24 Sturdee Avenue, Rosebank, Johannesburg 2196, South Africa

Penguin Books Ltd, Registered Offices:
80 Strand, London WC2R 0RL, England

First published in 2009 by Portfolio,
a member of Penguin Group (USA) Inc.

10   9   8   7   6   5   4   3   2   1

Copyright © George Whalin, 2009
All rights reserved

Photograph credits
Page 10: Photo provided by Jungle Jim's International Market; 21: © Gump's San Francisco; 29: © Archie McPhee & Company; 39, 85, 112, 124, 131, 140, 188, 209: Photos by George Whalin; 47: Abt Electronics; 60: Photo by Juan Lopez, courtesy of Zabar's; 68: © Bronner's CHRISTmas Wonderland; 77: Photo courtesy of Ron Jon Surf Shop; 96: Photo courtesy of ABC Carpet and Home; 104: In Celebration of Golf Inc.; 148: © 2008 Estes Ark ® The Look and Design of Estes Ark Is a Registered Trademark; 156: Junkman's Daughter; 162: Mark Gavron, Junkman's Daughter's Brother; 167: Smoky Mountain Knife Works; 174: Bering's; 181: Attila Aszodi; 195: © Copyright 2008 The Silver Queen Inc.; 201: Copyright Toy House, Inc., 2008

LIBRARY OF CONGRESS CATALOGING-IN-PUBLICATION DATA
Whalin, George.
  Retail superstars : inside the 25 best independent stores in America / George Whalin.
    p. cm.
  Includes index.
  ISBN 978-1-59184-260-6
  1. Stores, Retail—United States. 2. Retail trade—United States. I. Title.
  HF5429.3.W43 2009
  381'.11—dc22
                            2009001741

Printed in the United States of America
Set in Garamond No. 3
Designed by Sabrina Bowers

For Terri

I would be lost without you!

Contents

Two large chains dominate the twenty-first-century bookstore business, Borders and Barnes & Noble, with locations in cities across America. But in Portland, Oregon, book lovers prefer to shop Powell's City of Books over any other bookseller. In recent years, the number of locally owned bookstores has dwindled, while Powell's continues to thrive. It is today the world's largest independent seller of new and used books.

Abt, the most successful independent consumer electronics and appliance store in the nation, successfully competes in the brutal Chicagoland marketplace against all odds. This exquisitely designed and appointed suburban store sits on a thirty-seven-acre campus with parking for more than 1,000 cars. Abt sells consumer electronics and appliances from a vast array of well-known brands and is one of few manufacturer test sites for the newest appliances and electronics not yet on the market.

In a city filled with good food stores and delicatessens, Zabar's remains the one loved most by New Yorkers. This unpretentious store offers a tremendous variety of fish, kosher foods, breads, freshly ground coffee beans, vegetables, sweets, canned goods, and housewares. If you are looking for a massive selection of incredible foods, employees who really know their stuff, and an only-in-New York shopping experience, Zabar's won't disappoint.

Shoppers can find Christmas merchandise in an assortment of stores around the country. But there's only one Bronner's Christmas Wonderland and it's located in Frankenmuth, Michigan. Attracting more than three million shoppers a year, no other store comes close to Bronner's selection of Christmas merchandise. With 6,000 ornaments, 50,000 trims, and thousands of light sets, this is the world's largest Christmas store.

Small surf shops abound up and down both coasts, but only one is known as America's surfing mecca. Sporting a giant surfer atop its entrance, Ron Jon features a vast selection of surf equipment and apparel in a shop that can hardly be considered small. Attracting thousands of customers from all over the world each year, Ron Jon serves the needs of surfers and anyone who embraces the surfer lifestyle.

When one thinks of the best-known home furnishings destinations, the small town of Atchison, Kansas, isn't likely to show up on anyone's list. Yet, every year Nell Hill's attracts thousands of customers from Kansas City (more than an hour's drive away) and from cities and towns all across the Midwest. The constantly changing selection of truly unique home furnishings that cannot be found elsewhere delights shoppers.

LouisBoston opened in the 1920s as a pawnshop. The store and its knowledgeable staff now sell the finest-quality men's and women's apparel plus tasteful household items and gifts, all offered in an architecturally magnificent building. If you fear that elegance and style no longer exist in America, you will find it alive and well at LouisBoston.

Travelers driving toward the scenic Rocky Mountain community of Estes Park, Colorado, will discover an ark sitting alongside Highway 34. Unlike Noah's famous vessel, this ark won't float, but it is home to a very special toy store specializing in stuffed animals. In addition to selling a jaw-dropping assortment of teddy bears, it carries every kind of stuffed animal imaginable, from armadillos, jellyfish, and lizards to rhinoceroses, scorpions, and wolverines.

Many years ago Edwin Gavron's Big G Surplus was the place in Atlanta to go for closeout, overstock, and discontinued merchandise. Upon his retirement, his daughter opened a store of her own, selling everything from wigs and vintage apparel to costumes and memorabilia. She named her store Junkman's Daughter. Some time later her brother saw what fun she was having and opened Junkman's Daughter's Brother in the college town of Athens, Georgia. While both stores share the same heritage and have complementary names, they serve a different customer base and offer distinct selections of merchandise.

The town of Sevierville, Tennessee, best known as the gateway to the great Smoky Mountains, is home to the world's largest knife showplace. Knives of all kinds, along with collector and antique swords, outdoor equipment, watches, lighters, and books, fill this store top to bottom. With more than 1.2 million visitors a year,

Smoky Mountain Knife Works draws shoppers nationwide and from around the world.

chain stores focus on toys connected to movies and TV shows, Toy House carefully selects toys based on value, educational merit, and inherent ability to engage and delight children.

Retail Superstars

Introduction

For anyone who loves retailing, visiting hundreds of stores across the country each year would be a dream come true. For me it has been the perfect way to work and live my life. I love stores—big stores, medium-size stores, small stores—but most of all I love interesting, unique, one-of-a-kind stores. Although visiting stores is an important part of my job, it hardly seems like work. When I step into a creatively designed store, filled with a broad mix of interesting merchandise and staffed by friendly, attentive people, I delight in knowing I've found a retailer who "gets it."

Since 1987, I have traveled throughout the United States and around the world consulting with retailers and speaking at industry trade shows and corporate events. Everywhere I go, I visit stores. And I'm not done yet. My retail journey so far has been one great adventure after another, incredibly satisfying and just plain fun.

The idea for this book has been rattling around in my head for several years—long before the publication of *Retail Success,* my last book, which has been so widely read by retailers, consumer products manufacturers, and students of retailing. The book you now hold in your hands began to take shape in the late 1990s, spawned by an influx of calls from reporters seeking my thoughts on the perceived demise of independent retailing. The 1980s saw Wal-Mart opening stores in rural towns, resulting in thousands of small retailers' closing shop. In the 1990s, as Wal-Mart moved into larger communities, people both inside and outside the industry held Wal-Mart directly responsible for the so-called demise of independent retailing. Wal-

Mart's growth certainly contributed to the failure of weaker retailers, but the strong ones did just fine. And strong, well-run independent retail businesses continue to thrive today.

But this is not a book about Wal-Mart or how to compete against the giants, though the stores discussed are beating them. Several books already cover that topic quite well. *Retail Superstars* tells the story of twenty-five knock-your-socks-off stores and why customers love them. On the pages that follow you will find out what the people who own and manage the stores have done to achieve success and how their stores thrive in today's brutal retail marketplace. Savvy, innovative retailers with one-of-a-kind, dynamic stores not only survive in today's fiercely competitive environment but prosper as well.

I used two criteria in selecting the twenty-five stores featured in this book. The first was long-term success. The oldest of these stores opened in 1861 and the youngest in 1995. All have enjoyed considerable success throughout their histories. Second, the store had to be unique. That uniqueness could take several forms—an out-of-the-ordinary store design; an unusual, highly focused selection of merchandise; a business concept or philosophy clearly different from other retailers; or an exceptionally strong commitment to serving customers. Most of the stores I selected claim more than one of these uniqueness factors. A few have them all.

Each chapter relates some history of the store and background of its owners. Understanding the history paints a picture of how each store came to be and what it has taken to sustain its success. In some cases, people other than the founders influenced the store and its evolution. Other times unforeseen circumstances and events affected the choices made and the direction of the business. For some, being in the right place at the right time laid the groundwork for long-term success. Researching this book had plenty of surprises. I'll share them all with you.

As I interviewed the owners and talked with the people working in these one-of-a-kind stores, I discovered common characteristics and some startling differences. They all share an extraordinary passion for their businesses and an obsessive commitment to serving customers. It might be easy to say these retailers achieved great success because of such common characteristics, but that would be far too simplistic. Many factors played a part in the success of these stores and their ability to thrive among the dominant players of the modern retail world.

One of the most surprising revelations I found while researching and writing this book came up while interviewing the owners and chief executive officers of these stores. When asked whether their companies had been built based on a business plan or set of guidelines, they invariably answered no, their growth was guided by what customers wanted and expected from their stores, what the marketplace dictated, and how they could best serve their customers.

THE ASSAULT ON INDEPENDENT STORES

Being a healthy independent wasn't always such a retail phenomenon. Throughout America's early history until the late nineteenth century and early years of the twentieth century, retail stores were mostly single-location, family-owned businesses. In his book *Chain-Store Retailing 1859–1950,* Godfrey Lebhar describes the years when multiple-store operations such as Sears, Montgomery Ward, W. T. Grant, and JCPenney began spreading across America.

A few multistore companies existed before 1900, but chain stores really took off in the 1920s and '30s. In an attempt to stem the growth of chain stores, several communities and even states enacted laws to limit the number of new stores and stop the chains from expanding. As the country grew, these attempts to stop or slow the growth of chain stores failed.

After World War II, when the population boom fueled suburban growth, chain-store retailing became the norm and many downtown independents closed their doors. During the latter half of the twentieth century, thousands of independent retailers either went out of business or abandoned downtown locations and moved to the suburbs. At the same time, chain-store retailing flourished, giving consumers a great number of choices of where to shop.

Chain stores took over much of the retail landscape in America from that point on. Yet, a local backlash persists against massive superstores and the ongoing expansion of some national chains in various communities. A growing number of municipalities all across the country have passed or are considering local ordinances restricting the size of stores, particularly those over 100,000 square feet. Some local governments are even taking steps to keep national chains from opening in their communities altogether.

THE CONSUMER'S WORLD OF CHOICE

Businesses of all kinds compete for customer loyalty. While competition may be fierce in other business segments, it's brutal in retailing. Retailing has long been considered among the most competitive businesses in America. In the largest cities and suburbs, retailers frequently battle for customers facing competitors across the street, around the corner, or even next door. Visit any major shopping center: it's not unusual for several stores to carry the same brands. Dozens more sell comparable merchandise, all competing for the same consumer dollars. By every measure, far more stores exist in America than are necessary to serve the size of our population. In fact, the United States has significantly more stores per capita than any other country in the world.

Over the last thirty years, there has been explosive growth in the number and size of stores serving nearly every community, no matter its population. The sheer number of stores from which consumers have to choose today can be overwhelming. Big-box stores and warehouse clubs measuring in excess of 200,000 square feet are a common sight in small towns and big cities alike. Wal-Mart Supercenters loom large along rural highways and serve the needs of consumers for miles around. Giant warehouse clubs and massive superstores of all forms have changed where and how people shop in this country.

As this is being written, Wal-Mart operates more than 900 discount stores and nearly 2,600 supercenters (a combination discount store and supermarket), and it plans to open hundreds more stores each year for the foreseeable future. Family Dollar and Dollar General have a combined store count in excess of 14,200, with new stores opening daily. The Walgreen Company, with 6,500 drugstores, plans to build as many as 500 new stores a year for the next several years. Gap owns and operates more than 3,200 apparel stores under the Gap, Old Navy, and Banana Republic banners. The Safeway Company, comprising 1,700 supermarkets under five regional nameplates, recently started opening neighborhood convenience stores. Starbucks operates no less than 10,000 locations in the United States alone, with a stated goal of 15,000. Faced with too many stores in some communities and its goal of steady growth, Starbucks closed some of its stores in recent years that weren't generating sales at the level the company expected.

Every year the National Retail Federation names the Top 100 Retail Companies in America. In its most recent survey, the 100 largest U.S. retail companies operate 148,000 individual stores. Fluctuating fuel costs, the housing slump, an erratic stock market, and consumer malaise will force some chains to close poor-performing stores and temporarily slow the rate of expansion. For example, last year Lowe's opened 120 new stores with plans to decrease that number to 75 this year. International home furnishings retailer Ikea will open 10 to 15 new stores this year, down from its usual 20 to 25 openings in recent years. As the economy rebounds, so, too, will the pace and number of store openings.

Increasing market share to avoid giving ground to the competition remains the goal of the large retail chains as they add more and more stores. Unfortunately, just because a company can open new stores quickly does not mean the stores will run efficiently or serve consumers to their best advantage. In most cases, as the number of stores increases, customer service decreases. Unlike the stores profiled in this book, the largest retail chains generally do a poor job tailoring merchandise to a specific marketplace or to the people living in nearby communities.

There are those who lament the demise of neighborhood mom-and-pop stores that once served the needs of people in towns all across America. But mom-and-pop stores have not gone away; they simply have taken a different form. Today mom and pop operate such franchises as 7-Eleven, Easy Go, and Dairy Queen.

The stores profiled in this book bear no resemblance to the mom-and-pop stores of yesteryear. These are successful retail enterprises run by savvy merchants who know their businesses and how to grow and prosper in the most competitive retail climate in history.

THE OPPORTUNITY IN RETAILING

The nation's colleges and universities do a wonderful job educating young people to go into technology, science, medicine, the law, and other perfectly admirable professions. Only a few educate young retailers. Young people often pigeonhole the retail industry as one of hard work and long hours. They don't see the tremendous opportunities and incredibly rewarding career one can experience in retail.

The nation's largest retailers offer career opportunities not only for those interested in sales, but also for those trained in technology, sciences, and law. What the national chain stores can't offer is the opportunity to take an innovative concept and, through good old-fashioned hard work, create a one-of-a-kind retail business. In recent years we've seen some of that entrepreneurial zeal applied to online retailing. But many of the great retailers in this book embrace a more holistic approach to retailing, combining brick-and-mortar stores, catalogs, and Web sites to serve their customers.

Even in this time of overstoring, there continue to be real opportunities for forward-thinking independent retailers.

WHERE INDEPENDENT STORES THRIVE

We perceive big cities and suburbs as the breeding grounds for regional malls, power strip centers, and chain stores, but some of the best single-location stores started out and achieved great success in the nation's largest cities. New York City, with more than eight million inhabitants and a long culture of supporting neighborhood merchants, perfectly exemplifies a city supporting multiple independents. Other large cities where single-store retailers thrive include San Francisco, Houston, Los Angeles, and Chicago. Wonderful one-of-a-kind stores can also be found in very small communities. Atchison, Kansas; Estes Park, Colorado; and Hartville, Ohio, contributed home-grown treasures to this book. Consumers love to shop locally in stores with merchants who understand their needs.

THE BENEFITS OF BEING REMARKABLE

Faced with customer complaints and lost sales, a number of large retailers are exploring ways to improve the experience shoppers have in their stores. Self-checkout stations seem to be a popular solution to the problem of slow checkouts. This does speed up the process of getting out of the store, but not having to deal with some surly cashier proves to be the customer's real benefit. In every store in this book, associates truly care about serving the needs of their customers, and by doing so enhance the overall shopping experience.

In his bestselling book *The Big Moo,* Seth Godin and a group of well-respected business experts make a compelling case for creating a "remarkable" business, as opposed to doing the same things everyone else in business seems to be doing. Compared to so many cookie-cutter chain stores that all look alike and carry the same or similar merchandise, one can't help but acknowledge what these truly remarkable independent stores profiled herein have achieved.

When looking for a single word that best describes my select twenty-five, "distinguishable" hits the mark. These stores don't look the same, act the same, or carry the same merchandise. Some can't be missed because of the imaginatively designed buildings that house them. Walk through the doors and see interiors that will make you smile. Others offer truly incomparable selections of merchandise that can't be found in any other stores in the country. Some are classy, some are rowdy, some make your mouth water, and some take your breath away. The combination of all these characteristics makes them successful. In every case, the owners purposely created a shopping destination that underscores "remarkable" and certainly "distinguishable."

INNOVATION IS ALIVE AND WELL AMONG THESE RETAILERS

From coast to coast and border to border, one can drive down any major street and see many of the same stores, fast-food restaurants, and service businesses. This homogenization of American retail has become so pervasive, you can stand on a street corner in a host of cities and towns and not really know where you are. They all look the same. Countless communities all over America have lost the stores, restaurants, and local businesses that made them special.

Much has been written about innovative manufacturing companies such as Apple and Hewlett-Packard, but little acclaim goes out to innovative retailers. One must give credit to Target, Crate & Barrel, and Gap that all began with groundbreaking concepts. But copying is so common in retailing today that few retail concepts haven't been duplicated and integrated into other retail businesses soon after being introduced into the marketplace. When British retailer Tesco opened its first small-format Fresh & Easy food stores in Arizona, California, and Nevada, within a few weeks Wal-Mart and Safeway announced the opening of smaller-format stores—a blatant example of "me-tooing." Wal-Mart has gone so far as to open its Marketside stores in the suburbs of Phoenix, Arizona, where the first Fresh & Easy stores opened.

In this book you will read about some extraordinarily innovative retailers who continue to push the envelope, redefine their businesses, and try new things. You will read about Jim McIngvale who reinvents his extremely successful furniture business year after year, continuing to evolve, change, and get better. You'll learn what Jim Bonaminio does to ensure his food emporium remains incomparable to any other anywhere in the world. You will get a look into Michael Powell's book business, which breaks the mold of the traditional bookstore. You will learn how Mark Pahlow sells goofy novelties in Seattle, Washington, and turned his store into one of the favorite shopping destinations in that otherwise sophisticated community. Yes, retail innovation is alive and well and can be found among the retailers profiled in this book.

I hope you enjoy your journey through *Retail Superstars* and have as much fun reading about these stores as I have had finding them and bringing them all together. Don't forget to keep these stores in mind when you plan a trip. Every retailer and consumer products manufacturer, regardless of size or retail segment, can learn from these unparalleled merchants. Whether you are in the retail business or simply a person who loves shopping, you will thoroughly enjoy experiencing these unique stores in person.

Jungle Jim's
International Market

Fairfield, Ohio

Grocery shopping, a chore we all have to do, ranks right up there with filling the car with gasoline, mowing the lawn, and dusting the furniture. I don't know of anyone who jumps out of bed in the morning all fired up to go to the grocery store. That is, unless it's the day they get to go to Jungle Jim's International Market in Fairfield, Ohio.

SHOPPERTAINMENT

Attracting and keeping the attention of shoppers these days has become increasingly difficult, so retailers sometimes go to extreme measures. Take, for example, the nearly four dozen Bass Pro Shop's Outdoor Worlds around the United States. Each store features a huge glass-walled aquarium stocked with colorful fish. Visit American Girl Place in New York, Chicago, or Los Angeles, and you will find a restaurant and theater presenting live stage shows for their young customers. The newest Cabela's outdoor sports stores feature two-story mountains complete with trout ponds, waterfalls, and wild game displays. This type of retailing, dubbed shoppertainment, combines entertainment with shopping.

Some of the nation's food retailers have taken steps of late to improve the overall look of their grocery stores by widening aisles and installing subdued lighting, but few if any can be considered shoppertainment-oriented destinations, with one notable exception. The management team at Jungle Jim's International Market integrates delighting and amazing customers into their business culture. Jungle Jim's ranks right up there with the best shoppertainment retailers of the world.

Creating an inviting shopping destination in today's marketplace often means adding features that make the experience fun, exciting, and memorable for the customer. These features can include everything from animated characters like those seen in a Disney theme park to climbing walls like those found in REI's flagship stores. Such features serve the purpose of entertaining customers and keeping them in the store longer so they are likely to buy more of the store's merchandise.

At Jungle Jim's the experience begins before customers even enter the store. An actual oasis watering hole features animated, life-size elephants spouting water from their trunks, giraffes, cranes, and gorillas. Above the store's entrance hangs a colorful race car along with traffic lights by each door imprinted with START YOUR CARTS. The watering hole and the race car are just two of many entertainment-oriented features created solely to delight the store's customers.

THE MAN CALLED JUNGLE

Several of the retailers detailed in this book can be described as "characters," and Jim Bonaminio (better known as "Jungle" to his friends, associates, and customers) is among the most interesting of all. He often appears in the store dressed up in a wizard costume, safari suit, or fireman's uniform, to the amusement of his customers young and old. In a *BusinessWeek* article, he was described as "The Wizard of Odd." Jungle's approach to business may be unusual, but he's a wildly successful retailer with a business that cannot be compared to any other in the world. He works long hours every week, doing whatever it takes to ensure his customers are happy and his business continues to move forward.

As a strong proponent of differentiating his store from everyone else's, Jungle long ago learned the value of adding pizzazz to the shopping experience. This started while he was still in high school in Lorain, Ohio. An early business venture entailed buying a 1940s vintage bread truck, painting it yellow, and naming it the "Banana Wagon." Jungle made trips to Georgia and Florida, buying tomatoes, watermelons, and other fruits and vegetables that were out of season in Ohio. He brought them back in his Banana Wagon and sold them to people in Ohio eager for the otherwise unavailable produce.

FROM HUMBLE BEGINNINGS

Jungle Jim's International Market started in 1971 as a small, rural fruit-and-vegetable stand. A customer back in the early 1970s referred to Jim Bonaminio as "Jungle Man" and the name stuck. Having to relocate frequently in the early years, the original stand would best be described as semipermanent. In 1975, after the land was sold out from under his stand once again, Jungle bought his own piece of property nearby and built his first permanent fruit-and-vegetable stand. Calling it a store would be generous—it didn't actually have walls and was just 4,200 square feet. But it did have a roof—one made from recycled pickup truck camper shells.

Just inside the front door of Jungle Jim's today, one can see a portion of a pitched roof positioned under the much higher ceiling. This remnant came from the original fruit-and-vegetable stand. Photographs along the edge of this roof chronicle the evolution of the business as it grew and expanded over the years. These photos and the success of this impressive store attest to the hard work and dedication that went into building America's most captivating food emporium.

The checkerboard-like appearance of the store's ceiling reflects its many expansions over the years. Unlike typical retail construction, an assortment of recycled materials contributes to the decor of this one-of-a-kind store. As a dedicated bargain hunter and recycler, Jungle scours the countryside for pre-owned treasures that he cleans up, paints, and uses in the store. Among the most visible of these is the monorail track and its cars displayed at the front of the building. Jungle found the monorail at Ohio's Paramount Kings Island theme park. The goal is to one day run the monorail around the entire property. Jungle integrates his finds into the construction and decor throughout the store.

Today Jungle Jim's International Market is big—really big. To put the size in perspective, a typical American supermarket ranges from 35,000 to 40,000 square feet. The largest mass merchant's stores, such as a Wal-Mart Supercenter or Super Target, can be as large as 200,000 square feet. Jungle Jim's International Market measures an astounding 300,000 square feet. How about a one-hour guided tour? Not many stores offer guided tours, much less one that lasts a full hour. But with 300,000 square feet of food-shopping adventure, customers find it's absolutely worth taking the time.

FOODIELAND: A STORE FOR FOOD LOVERS

At Jungle Jim's, a paradise for foodies with more than 150,000 fresh and packaged foods from around the world, the selection in every department runs wide and deep. The Produce Department alone encompasses more space than an entire traditional grocery store.

A store this size with such a tremendous selection of merchandise attracts an abundance of shoppers. An estimated 50,000 people visit the store each week, traveling from hundreds of miles around. On any given day, automobile license plates representing as many as a dozen nearby states can be spotted in the parking lot.

Although a common practice in food stores, Jungle Jim's takes food sampling to a new level. In addition to the dozens of sampling stations positioned around the store, customers can sample virtually any item they want to try. All they need do is ask. If customers determine a particular variety of cheese, cracker, wine, ethnic food, or honey warrants a taste, the staff happily accommodates them.

With a passion for serving the needs of foodies, it is only natural for Jungle Jim's to incorporate a cooking school into the store. Carol Tabone, who has long managed the school, employs a staff of nine and regularly welcomes world-class guest instructors. The schedule of classes accommodates all skill levels—from beginners to gourmet cooks. A wide range of themed and specialty classes—Couples Cook Italian, Holiday Gifts from the Kitchen, Cooking a Stellar Candlelight Dinner—keeps the school curriculum fresh and makes it fun for experienced and aspiring chefs.

CHEESE, WINE, AND BEER

Variety, certainly the hallmark of this extraordinary store, becomes apparent in the Cheese Department, which stocks 1,600 varieties. Most people don't even know there are that many varieties of cheese. So you want a glass of wine with that cheese? Customers can choose from 12,000 vintage wines that range in price from inexpensive table wines to an $8,000 bottle of 2005 Domaine de la Romanée-Conti. The 30,000-square-foot Wine Department houses rack after rack of bottles from around the world, and a three-story, temperature-controlled wine cellar has the capacity for 3,000 cases of fine wine. In another of Jungle's finds, the bricks in the wine cellar date back to the 1800s, when they were used in an old stove factory. And the doors to the wine cellar come from an out-of-business produce company.

How can a customer choose from such a massive selection? Jungle Jim's conducts classes in wine selection, holds regular wine-tasting events, and hosts a wine club for the serious oenophile. Wine collectors can keep purchases in their own personal wine lockers provided in this area of the store. Special themed tastings in the wine cellar include Aromatic Whites, Great Wines for Grilling, West Coast Wines, Wines from South Africa, Bordeaux Bash, and Petite Syrah Mega-Event.

How about a beer? The Beer Department is something to behold, with a selection of more than 1,200 foreign and domestic varieties including several hundred microbrews. Beer lovers attend tasting events as enthusiastically as those who attend wine tastings.

FOODS FROM AROUND THE WORLD

These days it's not uncommon for supermarkets to stock a limited selection of ethnic foods to serve our broad tastes in food and diverse ethnic population. But Jungle Jim's goes beyond this. The ethnic foods at Jungle Jim's represent more than seventy-five countries. If a particular kind of food can't be found anywhere else in the United States, it can be found here. The customer who wants a hog's head for a special occasion can choose from at least a dozen. Cooks specializing in Chinese cuisine can find the most exotic ingredients to make their favorite dishes. Foreign-born shoppers who don't care for the Coke or Pepsi sold in the United States can buy the formulations sold in their countries.

Jungle Jim's also stocks the usual crackers and canned goods common in other stores, plus a wide array of imported items in these categories. Duck's feet, Amish chickens, ostrich eggs, blood oranges, banana flowers, bitter melon, lemongrass, an entire aisle of honey, thirteen varieties of grapefruit, eighty different olive oils, and thirty-two types of rice available in bags of up to fifty pounds give credence to the store's renown for the breadth of its assortments. Jungle and his buying staff believe in offering virtually unlimited choices, so they buy products from over 4,000 vendors around the world. This makes available an exotic and diverse selection of products that very likely will meet everyone's needs.

In the last several years the popularity of spicy foods and hot sauce has markedly increased in the United States among both native and foreign-born consumers. At Jungle Jim's, hot sauce is a big deal—a very big deal. There's mild for the faint of heart, moderate hot sauces, and little bottles of hot-sauce fire that come with written warnings. These can burn from the inside out. So just to make sure there aren't any mishaps, Jungle installed a full-size, antique fire engine atop the display (another recycled treasure). Many stores may think they have all the hot sauces anyone could want, but then they haven't seen Jungle Jim's 1,400 varieties.

The fire engine over the hot-sauce display impresses, but so do the forty-foot boat at the entrance to the Seafood Department and the seventeen-foot shark hanging over massive displays of fresh and frozen fish. Seafood lovers buy the freshest fish here short of casting their own lines. Glass tanks in this department allow customers to select still-swimming bass, trout, talapia, and live lobsters. The Live Fish Harvest area in the rear of the store houses huge tanks, and a 7,000-gallon water purification system maintains the stock of fresh seafood and fish.

VISUAL DYNAMICS LIKE NO OTHER

In his quest for the out-of-the-ordinary, Jungle's creations literally jam-pack the store with visual surprises. In addition to the oasis filled with animals outside and the race car above the entrance, a seven-foot-high mechanized lion entertains shoppers by singing Elvis Presley's "Jailhouse Rock." The Sherwood Forest display in English Foods comes complete with a talking Robin Hood. An antique Boar's Head truck hangs above the Deli. A full-size rickshaw sits in Chinese Foods along with a colorful three-wheeled taxi that might be found on the streets of an Indian city. Other delights include an Amish horse-drawn buggy in Meats and Coney Island bumper cars filled with sweets in the Candy Department.

The props can also be a bit bizarre. Two men's and women's Porta Potties situated in the front area of the store look as though they belong on a construction site rather than in a food store. But they are false fronts, and once through the doors, customers find themselves in beautifully appointed restrooms. These creative facilities were recognized as "America's Best Restroom" in the sixth annual competition sponsored by Cintas Corporation, a supplier of restroom cleaning and hygiene products.

Just inside the front door, a five-and-a-half-foot-tall Campbell's Soup can perched on a seventeen-foot-high swing set was originally installed to celebrate National Soup Month. The animated soup can sings, talks, and swings back and forth as it chats with children in the store.

A small theater in the rear of the store runs a video presentation chronicling Jungle Jim's life and success story. The Oscar Event Center, where customers can hold private parties and other special events, comfortably handles large groups (up to 850 people) as well as smaller gatherings (fewer than 100 people).

AN EXCEPTIONAL GROCERY STORE

Over the years Jungle Jim's has established itself as *the* destination for diverse foods from all over the world. But it also stocks a massive selection of the type of food and merchandise one expects to find in any American grocery store. This includes a sprawling array of fresh fruits and vegetables, a huge Frozen Foods section, an Organic Foods Department, Paper Goods, Pet Department, amazing Deli, and top-notch Bakery that wafts tantalizing smells throughout the store.

In addition to the meats one expects to find, the Meat Department claims its own uniqueness and vast selection, including kosher meats, more than twenty kinds of homemade sausages, free-range chickens, and not-so-common meats such as ostrich, rattlesnake, and elk. It doesn't stop there. Other standard stocked items include heads from pigs and cows along with feet from ducks and chickens.

In recent years Jungle Jim's has undergone some structural changes, the most momentous of which is the 85,000-square-foot addition built up front. Negotiating a 300,000-square-foot food emporium can be daunting if one wants to quickly run in and pick up a few groceries. In an effort to better serve the needs of local customers, this addition works much like a store within a store, housing American Groceries along with the Deli, Sushi, Cheese, Wine, and Beer departments. Other enhancements geared to the local shopper include a Starbucks, branches of the Fifth Third Bank and U.S. Post Office, Cincinnati Bell store, large pharmacy, and an eyeglass dispenser. The Seasonal Department just outside the front door serves as a garden center and gift shop in the warmer months and a Christmas shop during the holidays.

DEFYING TRADITIONAL THINKING

Defying the widely held rule of retailing success—the importance of a convenient location—Jungle Jim's sits four miles from the nearest major freeway. The community of Fairfield, Ohio, while considered a suburb of Cincinnati, hardly can be called a close suburb. The drive to Jungle Jim's from the most populous areas of the city often requires negotiating the common big-city traffic nightmares. In spite of all that, the store attracts thousands of customers every week from Cincinnati and around the Midwest—a true destination.

Why is this? It's partly due to the hard work and long hours put in by its charismatic owner and dedicated staff. But Jungle's extraordinary success comes first and foremost from his strategic decision to build an absolutely unique destination in a marketplace filled with me-too stores. Even in today's highly competitive retail environment, it would be impossible for another retailer to duplicate the look, shopping experience, or breadth of merchandise available at Jungle Jim's.

The retailers profiled in this book all feel strongly about supporting their communities. They're good citizens and Jungle is no exception. Long before he became a successful retailer, he was an accomplished athlete, playing baseball in high school and college. He now shares his love of sports by sponsoring more than 200 local teams. His compassion goes beyond sports. One Way Farm, a shelter for abused and troubled teens, is just one of the other community organizations that benefits from Jungle's largess.

THE CHALLENGE FOR GROCERS

Major supermarket chains operate hundreds of stores in communities all across the country. Safeway, Kroger, Albertson's, Ralphs, Wegmans, Food Lion, Harris-Teeter, H-E-B, ALDI, Fred Meyer, and dozens of other grocers all operate successful regional chains. Wal-Mart, Costco, and Target claim a percentage of the grocery business these days as well. Yet Jungle Jim's, with its single location, amazing selection of merchandise, and wonderful shopping experience continues to grow and prosper, drawing customers from hundreds of miles around. There may be lots of places to buy food, but there's only one Jungle Jim's International Market.

Some retailers resist making frequent or big changes; Jungle Jim's makes change a part of its business strategy. New merchandise, new features, new displays, and new customer attractions keep the store fresh and interesting. Jungle Jim's International Market epitomizes what it takes to stand out and attract customers in today's fiercely competitive retail marketplace.

JUNGLE JIM'S INTERNATIONAL MARKET

5440 DIXIE HIGHWAY

FAIRFIELD, OHIO 45014

(513) 674-6000

WWW.JUNGLEJIMS.COM

MORE PHOTOS OF JUNGLE JIM'S CAN BE SEEN AT
WWW.RETAILSUPERSTARS.COM/JUNGLEJIMS.

Gump's

San Francisco,
California

Few businesses last 148 years. **Fewer yet last that long** having endured major earthquakes, fires, and several ownership changes. Just one of these plights might have destroyed a weaker, less respected enterprise than Gump's. But Gump's endured and today sells distinctive merchandise to San Francisco's elite as it has for nearly a century and a half.

In addition to its legendary store on Post Street near renowned Union Square, this extraordinary retail business produces a first-class mail-order catalog and uses the Web to reach even more customers. All three retail venues sell Gump's exclusives that cannot be found elsewhere. This company embraces today's multichannel retailing environment, serving customers equally well whether they choose instore, catalog, or online shopping.

A HISTORY LIKE NO OTHER

In 1861, coinciding with the explosive population growth in Northern California and vast personal wealth spawned from California's Gold Rush, brothers Solomon and Gustav Gump opened S & G Gump. The brothers sold paintings, art objects, mirrors with gilded frames, and other items that appealed to the discriminating tastes of newly wealthy San Franciscans. Much of this merchandise, particularly the paintings of voluptuous nudes, found their way into the city's saloons and bordellos as well.

The famous 1906 earthquake with an estimated magnitude of nearly 8.0 destroyed the Gump's store on Geary Street and devastated much of San Francisco in the early morning hours of April 18. When Solomon was able to reopen, he turned over management of the business to his son A. L. Gump. This plump, jovial man would run the store well into the 1940s. During his tenure, he made significant changes in the store's offerings, expanding into imported Oriental art and jewelry. The selections of Oriental art, home accessories, and jewelry at Gump's remain unparalleled to this day.

By the time A.L. died in 1947, his son Richard ran the day-to-day operations. As an astute buyer, Richard Gump carried forth, refining the store's offerings in order to satisfy the sophisticated and changing tastes of his customers. Following the end of World War II, tourists poured into San Francisco, further cementing Gump's esteem among the world's best stores for high-quality jewelry, art, home furnishings, and gifts.

Mail order as a way of doing business gained momentum across America in the early 1950s, which is when Gump's introduced its first catalog. The mail-order catalog proved the perfect way to keep Gump's merchandise at the fingertips of all those tourists to San Francisco who had fallen in love with the store. The catalog became a substantial contributor to Gump's success over the years.

Like many single-store retail businesses, Gump's moved around a lot as it grew during those early years. Ultimately the store settled in at 250 Post Street, where it remained for much of the twentieth century, a destination for discerning shoppers looking for elegant merchandise from around the world. Then, in the early 1990s, Gump's moved down the street into the first two stories of a building at 135 Post Street, where it can be found today.

The latter years of the twentieth century saw Gump's change hands several times. Unfortunately, the store suffered from several years of neglect and merchandising philosophies that differed from owner to owner. Ultimately it became the property of Hanover Direct, a mass-market catalog company best known for moderately priced apparel and home goods. In what was no surprise to retail pundits, Hanover Direct and Gump's turned out to be a poor fit. This became quite evident when Hanover added cheap gift merchandise to the formerly exclusive Gump's catalog.

In 2005, after Hanover Direct nearly destroyed Gump's, a private investor group came to the rescue with the intention of reviving the brand and restoring the luster to this famous retail enterprise. To their credit, the store, catalog, and Web site once again live up to the standards set by the Gump family while continuing to reflect the excellent tastes of its customers.

The best business strategy for specialty retailers has always been one that produces legions of delighted customers who love and enjoy everything they buy so much that they can't wait to visit the store again and again. In this regard, Gump's excels and enjoys a sterling reputation with well-heeled San Franciscans and tourists alike who appreciate top-quality, out-of-the-ordinary giftware, jewelry, and home goods. Gump's nurtures these relationships over the long term

with a good number of customers who have remained loyal generation after generation.

A TOUR OF GUMP'S

Gump's clearly proves its merchandising prowess in its extraordinary
first-floor jewelry displays. Pearls of every size, shape, and color and
necklaces, earrings, rings, and brooches inlaid with jade, coral, diamonds, and other gemstones fill the glass cases. An array of jade exhibits not only pieces designed with the traditional rich green stones
but also the lesser-known white and black. Lovely coral jewelry shows
a variety of color as well. One can choose from the familiar light orange or an assortment of deep red and pure white. A necklace coupling green jade stones with white pearls surrounding is one example
of the exquisite pieces designed using gemstone combinations that
can't help but entice jewelry lovers.

Not only does Gump's offer a breadth of jewelry choices, it also
offers truly unique jewelry. When I asked about Gump's distinctive
jewelry pieces, Marilu Klar, vice president of jewelry, replied, "We
don't do what everybody else does." In a marketplace filled with too
many stores selling the same or similar merchandise, being distinctive proves to be the best way for a single-store retailer to separate itself from the crowd. While every jewelry store in town sells watches
and traditional bridal jewelry, Gump's avoids these merchandise categories for that very reason.

In addition to jewelry, first-floor shoppers can browse decorative
vases, bowls, and jars, as well as wall and floor screens in traditional
oriental and contemporary designs. Mirrors, prints, and framed art
pieces can also be found in this part of the store. Decorating accessories such as pillows and throws interspersed throughout the store add
to the overall warmth of the decor. With a long history of displaying
original works of art, Gump's holds regular shows spotlighting great
art and artists. The first floor houses the gallery of fine artwork from
current featured artists.

In the center of the store, strategically placed near the staircase, sits a large Ching Dynasty gilded wood Buddha that seems to keep watch over all who pass by. A gallery of Limoges collectibles, decorating pieces for the office, the Custom Stationery Department, and a choice of books on art, culture, and architecture can be found tucked in an area behind the staircase. Home fragrances, a recent addition, rounds out the first floor. Gump's three exclusive signature scents come in diffusers, interior colognes, candles, and scented stones.

On the second floor, Gump's achieves what few retailers are capable of these days. It presents an extensive selection of high-end tabletop merchandise from the premier brands and designers in such categories as flatware, stemware, and dinnerware. Better-quality department stores once did well with this category, but most have opted not to carry the high-end goods. Today, it takes a store like Gump's to make available such a wide array of top-of-the-line tabletop pieces.

As though stepping into a gallery of the finest works of art, Gump's second floor affords the opportunity to buy crystal stemware by Baccarat and Waterford, sterling silver flatware from Christofle and Reed & Barton, classic dinnerware from Wedgwood, and contemporary style dinnerware from Hermes. Beautifully crafted pieces of flatware come from Italian designer Gianmaria Buccellati. Like Buccellati's delicately elegant jewelry, experts consider each piece of Buccellati flatware a work of art itself.

A variety of furniture pieces, area rugs, accessories, lighting, and linens fill out the second floor.

AN EXPERIENCED RETAIL PROFESSIONAL

Not long after the venture-capital firm purchased Gump's, the new owners saw the wisdom in consolidating catalog, online, and store buyers into one cohesive unit. The benefits? A single group of buyers with a shared vision brings about merchandise consistency among the three areas as well as cost savings. Another smart move was to recruit retail professional Marta Benson to head up the business. Marta spent a number of years learning the retail business at two successful lifestyle companies before coming to Gump's. After eight years at Smith & Hawken, Paul Hawken's store and catalog business that sells merchandise for the home and garden, she moved on to Restoration Hardware. There she held key management positions, first merchandising the store, then launching the company's catalog and online business, and later becoming responsible for merchandising and marketing all channels of the $700 million home brand.

Of the many skills Marta brings to Gump's, her thorough understanding of protecting, nurturing, and leveraging a well-known and highly respected brand may be the most valuable. Both Smith & Hawken and Restoration Hardware do an excellent job of building and leveraging their brands in a highly competitive marketplace.

The Gump's brand had been built up for more than 140 years before it was neglected and even tarnished at times. Under Marta's direction and guidance, the brand once again stands alone. The value of the Gump's brand becomes evident when hearing the many stories of customer loyalty to the store and staff loyalty to customers. Marilu Klar recounts one such story about a couple who were about to celebrate their fiftieth wedding anniversary. Gump's played an important role in the celebration, first by making a very special ring for the matriarch. The couple, having booked passage for their entire family on an Alaskan cruise, also wanted to surprise each of their children and grandchildren with a special gift from Gump's for the occasion. Since Gump's and a particular salesperson had enjoyed a relationship with the family for so long, the couple secretly decided to bring the salesperson to the celebration for the evening of their anniversary. While the family was out for the day, the salesperson surreptitiously boarded the ship where she placed the gifts for each person on the dinner table. They all loved the gifts, and were delighted to see their favorite Gump's salesperson on board.

Another Gump's phenomenon occurs when salespeople alert regular customers of special pieces of jewelry that have recently arrived in the store. Trusting the store and the salespeople's taste, invariably customers will buy pieces sight unseen and have them delivered. Of course, customers can return the pieces if they don't care for them, but that is the exception. The rapport between good customers and their favorite salespeople develops over time and after a while the salespeople know just what their customers will love to own. The relationships between Gump's salespeople and the customers they serve for many years count among the store's most valuable assets.

CREATING AN ICON

I doubt the brothers Gump set out all those many years ago to create an American retailing icon, but that is exactly what happened. From selling mirrors and gaudy art to saloons and brothels to providing the finest luxury brands to sophisticated shoppers worldwide proved quite a journey. Many people contributed to the success of Gump's. Even with difficulties along the way, throughout Gump's history the vision and commitment required to carefully choose just the right merchandise and present it in a classic, elegant setting has remained steadfast and has played a major role in Gump's longevity.

Gump's maintains its status as one of San Francisco's great institutions. It's a rare day that doesn't find tourists perusing the treasures that can be found only there. Curb appeal doesn't hurt either, with large, inviting windows fronting the store, aesthetically pleasing to passersby. While Gump's may be famous for its luxury merchandise, tourists and Bay Area residents can find beautiful, moderately priced items as well. A wide selection of tasteful merchandise is priced under $100. When customers visit this wonderful store, more often than not they find something they can't live without. There's nothing quite like San Francisco's Gump's.

GUMP'S

135 POST STREET

SAN FRANCISCO, CA 94108

(415) 982-1616

WWW.GUMPS.COM

MORE PHOTOS OF GUMP'S CAN BE SEEN AT

WWW.RETAILSUPERSTARS.COM/GUMPS.

Archie McPhee

Throughout this book such words as "unusual," "spectacular," and "fabulous" appropriately describe the stores featured herein. In the case of Archie McPhee and its bizarre mix of merchandise, these words don't do justice. "Quirky," "zany," "goofy," or "irreverent" might work better, but this store and its merchandise are as close to indescribable as any you'll ever find. First-time customers can't possibly anticipate what they'll experience when approaching the rather nondescript building that houses this retail enterprise. Walk through the doors and it's an entirely different story. The merchandise and its presentation prove anything but ordinary. Archie McPhee, founded and owned by Mark Pahlow, sells novelty items of a sort that make for a delightful shopping adventure. Not everything sold in this store warrants the quirky, zany, or goofy tag, but the combination of all the merchandise makes shopping Archie McPhee so appealing.

This store caters to people who like to laugh, aren't sensitive or easily offended, and find that a little irreverence is good for the soul. In fact, if you have a bent toward political and social correctness, you might want to skip this chapter.

WHO WAS ARCHIE MCPHEE?

In 1924, young Archie McPhee and the North Star Music Makers, a Minnesota-based band he managed, set out on the SS *President Madison* to share their love of jazz with the people of the Orient. The SS *President Madison* had hired the North Star Music Makers to be its house band, but when Archie and the musicians arrived on board, it was discovered that accommodations had not been reserved for Archie. The ship had an opening for a coal stoker, which Archie chose to take to avoid being left behind. Throughout the voyage he worked at his coal tender job and performed his duties as band manager. Coincidently the SS *President Madison* was based in Seattle, Washington, destined one day to be the home of the Archie McPhee namesake store

Many years later, Mark Pahlow married Archie's great-niece and found the family's stories of his wife's uncle—the fun-loving adventurer with an entrepreneurial spirit—captivating. Mark, an entrepreneur himself, sold rubber chickens and other novelty items out of his home in Los Angeles. In 1983, believing the Northwest would be a better market for such an enterprise, he rented a U-Haul, packed up, moved to Seattle, and named the fledgling retail enterprise to honor his inspiring great-uncle-in-law.

As the business grew, Mark moved his store several times before settling into Seattle's Ballard neighborhood. After a while, he needed even more space and expanded across the parking lot into what had once been a liquor store. He named that part of the store "More Archie McPhee." Now twenty-six years old and a Seattle retail landmark, Archie McPhee attracts 80,000 visitors a year from all over who come to see what makes this store special.

Originally the store sold some of the same quirky novelty items still stocked today, but it served as a surplus store more than anything else, selling merchandise from a variety of sources. The change came about as Mark expanded the exclusive novelty merchandise conceived in-house by Mark and his creative staff. This expansion also spawned the company's wholesale business, Accoutrements. Today Mark and his staff operate a diverse business composed of the Archie McPhee store, several active Web sites, the retail catalog, and Accoutrements, which wholesales its creations to other novelty and gift stores. Archie McPhee even has a bridal registry.

THE MERCHANDISE

Nice, friendly, interesting people work in the store, but Archie McPhee is all about the merchandise. Goofy, saucy, celebratory, and funny, the merchandise stars here. Shana Iverson, store manager, and David Wahl, Internet marketing and PR manager, call it "impractical necessities," particularly when describing what Accoutrements creates for the store, catalog, and Web site.

The Stupid Products category encompasses such can't-live-without treasures as the World's Largest Underpants, Yodeling Pickles, Cowboy Boot Sideburns, and Inflatable Toast. Bandages à la Archie McPhee go way beyond the plain sterile strip or cute cartoon-adorned kids' varieties. The injured of all ages can cheer themselves up with a wild assortment of bandages designed to look remarkably like bacon strips, fried eggs, pickles, pirate flags and skulls, toasted slices of bread, monkey faces, crime scene tape, and lips in assorted colors puckered and ready to kiss the boo-boo. A Beef Bandage Assortment enables meat lovers to make a statement—one who sports a T-bone steak bandage deserves notice.

The Zombies & Monsters category provides a fine selection of Zombie-Brain Gelatin Molds, a Glow-in-the-Dark Flesh-Eating Zombies Play Set, and a set of sixteen Deluxe Finger Monsters. Devil Duckies, a corruption of the classic yellow rubber ducks children enjoy playing with in the bathtub, come in red and black with devil horns growing from their cute little heads. Jumbo Devil Duckies, Ninja Devil Duckies, Glow Zombie Devil Duckies, Camo Devil Duckies, and a tub of 144 Mini Devil Duckies round out this category.

Archie McPhee devotes an entire category to Jesus and other religious icons for those who have a sense of humor about religion. There's the Dashboard Jesus that mounts on a spring so it functions like a bobble-head doll, Jesus Air Freshener, Lord's Prayer Singing Alarm Clock, and several action figures, including Moses and Pope Innocent III.

Archie McPhee excels at action figures. Its considerable inventory maintains likenesses not done by any other action figure company. One can buy singular action figures or complete play sets. Historical figures include such notables as Sigmund Freud, Ben Franklin with kite and key, Sherlock Holmes, Alexander the Great, and Marie Antoinette complete with chopped-off head. Also represented are Lunch Lady, reminiscent of net-headed cafeteria servers; Crazy Cat Lady and her six cats; Big Foot, which leaves footprints from the rubber stamps on the bottom of his feet and the included stamp pad; and Obsessive Compulsive, decked out in face mask and handy moist towelette. One of my favorite action figures depicts Seth Godin, the well-known author and speaker who writes and comments about marketing and business strategies.

Customers get a kick out of the Our Weirdest Products category into which almost all of the store's products seem to fit. But items designated "The Weirdest" include a Windup Hopping Lederhosen, Ceramic Smoking Baby, Corn Dog Air Freshener, seventeen-inch Latex Vulture, Pig Acupuncture Model, Nunzilla the windup nun that shoots sparks from her mouth, and a box of twenty-four wa-termelon-flavored lollipops that come in the shape of Sigmund Freud's head.

In addition to the categories already mentioned, the follow-ing will spur your imagination: Catapults, Candy, The Cubes, Uni-corns & Ninjas, Poker, Hula, Costumes, Monkeys, Office/School Supplies, Cocktail Supplies, Cowboy, Kitchen, Sushi, Evil, McPhee T-Shirts, and Archie's Attic.

Throughout the store, dump bins and displays contain a variety of uncategorized goods, such as small plastic animals, Seven Deadly Sins wristbands, stickers of all kinds, Gummy products including an Anatomical Gummy Heart, Bacon-Flavored Toothpicks, Last Supper After Dinner Mints, and the eye bin with its wide variety of glass taxidermy eyes. The store's selection focuses on out-of-the-ordinary novelty items instead of the usual fake barf and doggie doo that are so readily available in other novelty stores.

The Archie McPhee product creation team and buyers live by the maxim, "Go for the obvious joke. If it's funny, it's got a chance."

AN AMAZING SHOPPING EXPERIENCE

The merchandise certainly takes center stage at Archie McPhee, but supporting characters and features add to the entertainment aspect of shopping there. If the merchandise alone cannot entertain a shopper, Motog the Talking Tiki and Captain Archie Fortune Teller, reminis-cent of the animated games once found on carnival midways, cer-tainly will.

Customers also get a kick out of snapping photos alongside the eight-foot Gladiator statue and the Captain Archie cutout, behind which they stand, insert their heads, and pose as the legendary sea-faring adventurer. The photo booths of yesteryear that once were found in shopping centers, bus depots, and roller rinks across America entice shoppers to squeeze in as many companions as possible, have their picture taken, and await the strip of black-and-white photos developed after a few minutes. The photo quality is lacking and the strip smells of chemicals, but the appeal never ceases.

In the rear of the store stands Archie's Wall of Fame, displaying photos, letters, and notes from many of the celebrities who have visited the store. And then there's the famed Giant Devil Head, which frequently gets redecorated to reflect the time of year or season. The Giant Devil Head claims a history of great renown.

THE POWER OF MEDIA RELATIONSHIPS

One day after the last coat of paint had been applied to the Giant Devil Head, it was placed outside the back door to dry. When store personnel went to retrieve it, it was gone. Someone had stolen it. Being so well known in the community, the folks at Archie McPhee let it be known to customers and friends that the Giant Devil Head had gone missing. Soon the story took on a life of its own. Local newspapers and radio and TV stations reported on the stolen Giant Devil Head. The store just wanted it back and encouraged the thieves to return it with no questions asked. After several weeks, someone realized that the devil's head he had bought elsewhere and planned to use as a party decoration was actually the one stolen from Archie McPhee. He immediately contacted the store, but he had no way to return it because of its size. The Archie McPhee truck picked it up. As it was being driven back to the store, people along the route cheered the return of the Giant Devil Head.

The theft of the Giant Devil Head resulted in thousands of dollars' worth of free media coverage for the store. Although this publicity wasn't initiated by Archie McPhee, the staff nurtures its all-important relationship with Seattle's media.

At one time the Ballard neighborhood, where the store is located, was a separate city from Seattle. Every year the store holds a Free Ballard Day event to commemorate when the town was annexed by the city of Seattle. The event receives lots of media attention, and

Archie McPhee provides bumper stickers and other items. The annexation of Ballard occurred more than 100 years ago so it's unlikely anyone actually remembers the day it happened. But the celebration makes for a fun event for Archie McPhee and Ballard residents.

The store rarely uses traditional advertising, but instead holds several in-store events each year, including a big sidewalk sale in July, an annual blood drive, costume contests, and a major celebration for Halloween. The staff wears different costumes every day during the week-long Halloween festivities, and customers dress up as well, to participate in the various activities planned throughout the week. Photos of all these events get posted on Flickr.com for everyone to enjoy.

CELEBRATING AND SUPPORTING LOCAL HEROES

Every big city claims its local heroes and celebrities, and Seattle is no different. Nancy Pearl, a Seattle librarian, ranks very high on their celebrity list. As a champion of reading, she thought up the idea of a whole community reading one book; she developed the program "If All of Seattle Read the Same Book." Since its inception in 1998, cities throughout the United States have adopted the program to encourage people to read. Nancy Pearl has since become a different sort of celebrity. The *New York Times* calls her "the talk of librarian circles." But two other things helped establish her fame—the monthly television program *Book Lust with Nancy Pearl* and the Nancy Pearl action figure from Archie McPhee.

Publicity prior to the introduction of the Nancy Pearl action figure rankled some librarians, irritated at the prospect of their profession being stereotyped, most likely because of the shushing sound made by the Nancy Pearl action figure when the button on her back is pushed. In spite of that, orders poured in and more than 2,000 Nancy Pearl action figures shipped the first day. Oddly enough, many of those orders came from librarians. Immortalizing this well-respected and nationally known librarian turned out to be a good thing for both Nancy Pearl and Archie McPhee. The regular and deluxe librarian action figures continue to be bestsellers.

Seattle also claims a celebrity from the past. As was done in many cities in the 1950s and '60s, Seattle produced a local afternoon television show for children hosted by a clown. Seattle's *J.P. Patches* TV show ran from 1958 to 1981. With such a long-running show, thousands of Seattle children grew up loving J.P. Patches. It was only natural for Archie McPhee to create a J.P. Patches action figure. Grown-up fans of the clown buy the action figure likeness as a fond remembrance from their childhoods.

USING SOCIAL MEDIA AND AN INTERESTING WEB SITE TO ENGAGE CUSTOMERS

Social media Web sites such as Flickr and YouTube play increasingly important roles in establishing massive online communities that benefit individuals as well as savvy business owners. In this new media environment there may not be another retailer, large or small, that more effectively engages its customers using these tools than Archie McPhee. By encouraging customers to use a broad group of Web sites, Archie McPhee has become one of the most mentioned retail businesses on the Web. For example, Archie McPhee's photostream on Flickr includes hundreds of photos showing customers in the store, various Archie McPhee products, catalog pages, and staff photos. Social networking site Yelp provides customers the opportunity to post reviews of the store and its products. YouTube visitors can view some interesting and creative television commercials and videos made by Archie McPhee customers using the store's products. Wikipedia, the free encyclopedia Web site, tells the Archie McPhee story. An especially amusing photo shows two people from the Travel Channel, who were there to produce a feature piece on the store, trying on the World's Largest Underpants, both at the same time.

As an early advocate of the Internet, Archie McPhee first appeared on the Web in 1996. The constantly changing, visually dynamic, easy-to-navigate Web site allows visitors to browse the massive Archie McPhee merchandise selection and securely buy online. They can also see store photos, receive merchandise recommendations from individual staff members, and obtain a coupon for free stuff in the store. The coupon changes every month so visitors frequently come back for a new coupon.

The Web site displays photos of its party merchandise offered for rental in and around the Seattle area. Where else can you rent a Giant Pop Out Cake that can hide a man or woman who pops out for a birthday or other occasion? One can rent a pair of Giant Scissors for ribbon-cutting ceremonies, large dried Palm Trees, Disco Mirror Balls, or Fog Machines.

Archie McPhee mails approximately 250,000 copies of its catalog annually. Each item's description tells a little story of how the product can be used. The copywriting, like the store, shows a wonderful sense of humor. If the products themselves don't make you laugh, the descriptions will. Unlike some other retailers, Archie McPhee uses its catalog primarily to drive customers to its Web site. It's much more costly these days to produce and mail catalogs, whereas Web sites, once established, can instantly be updated and afford retailers a much farther reach. At the same time, catalogs still play an important role keeping in touch with customers, even if it is to simply bring them to the company's Web site.

SUCCESS FROM BIZARRE MERCHANDISE, A FUN SHOPPING EXPERIENCE, AND WORD OF MOUTH

Word-of-mouth Internet style allows consumers to easily share with others what they like and don't like about almost anything—quality of merchandise, speed of delivery, easy return policies, and the like. For a retailer like Archie McPhee with one store, this by-product of the cyber age proves quite advantageous. An Internet search will show lots of positive comments about Archie McPhee, assuring those who know the company only from its Web site or catalog that it's reputable.

One of the things I find most refreshing about this company is its willingness to try new things without a fear of failure. While the Yodeling Pickle was a hit, My Pretty Nose Hair failed. Every year brings new products. Some sell well, some don't. Trying new things without fearing failure is a great attribute for any company, particularly one that counts on bringing customers back again and again.

Archie McPhee makes people laugh—tears rolling down the face kind of laughter. A visit to this store provides a delightful respite from the ordinary chores in our lives. And if you want to witness a successful retail enterprise that doesn't subscribe to traditional business methods, you won't find a better example.

Later this year Archie McPhee expects to move to a new location in the Wallingford neighborhood of Seattle. The address will be 1300 N. Forty-fifth Street.

ARCHIE MCPHEE
2428 NW MARKET STREET
SEATTLE, WASHINGTON 98107
(206) 297-0240
WWW.ARCHIEMCPHEESEATTLE.COM

MORE PHOTOS OF ARCHIE MCPHEE CAN BE SEEN AT
WWW.RETAILSUPERSTARS.COM/ARCHIEMCPHEE.

Powell's City of Books

Portland, Oregon

The competitive environment for independent bookstores has been extremely challenging over the last several years. In the early 1990s more than 4,000 independent
bookstores belonged to the American Booksellers Association. Today fewer than 1,200 belong. Each year more
and more independents close their doors, including such
well-known, long-established stores as WordsWorth Books
in Cambridge, Massachusetts; Coliseum Books in New
York City; and Cody's Books in Berkeley, California.

Most blame the demise of these independent booksellers on the explosive growth of national chains such as Barnes & Noble and Borders, plus Amazon's remarkable online success. Also at fault are the changing habits and tastes of Americans as they forgo reading in favor of television, video games, and surfing the Net. While the nation's book lovers continue to buy lots of books, a startling number of Americans do not read a single book in a year.

In the midst of all this doom and gloom, one independent bookstore shines. Powell's in Portland, Oregon, the world's largest independent seller of new and used books, operates its exceptional City of Books, several small specialty bookstores around the city, and a Web site that rivals the best in the book business.

A REALLY BIG BOOKSTORE

Powell's City of Books covers an entire city block on Burnside Street in downtown Portland. National chain store merchants tend to take a narrow view of the book business, defining their customer base as those living within a few-mile radius of the individual stores. Their inventory focus leans toward recently published titles, bestsellers, and a few backlisted books. Powell's City of Books, being a profoundly different kind of book business, takes a more global outlook on selling books, as is attested to by its massive selection of 4.5 million titles between the store and its Web site. Powell's displays both new and used hardbacks and paperbacks side by side so customers can choose without going to a separate part of the store for one or the other. Book lovers whose first language may not be English can find a comprehensive assortment of titles in many of the world's languages. Those searching for an out-of-print or rare book have a better than average chance of finding it at Powell's.

Powell's is neither the slickest nor the most dynamic store you will ever see, but it is one of the most comfortable. A feeling of tranquillity and warmth exists that too often gets lost in overly designed stores. It is what a bookstore should be—stress free. Shoppers can be found browsing through the massive selection in every corner of the store. And with eight rooms of books spread over three floors, there are quite a few corners. It's common to find people sitting cross-legged on the floor paging through books, and they can do so for as long as they want without any pressure to buy. Exploring a store like this makes a favorite pastime for those of us who treasure books. To accommodate its patrons, this book lover's paradise stays open 365 days a year from 9 A.M. until 11 P.M.

Powell's categorizes its books into more than 150 sections and 1,000 subsections and provides a color-coded map of the store to help customers navigate through it all. If the map doesn't do it, knowledgeable associates are on hand to help customers find what they want and suggest other books they might enjoy.

Bookstores frequently host author appearances, but unlike other stores, Powell's integrates author appearances, readings, and book discussion groups into its schedule nearly every day of the week. These events prove to be quite an effective marketing tool. Powell's also publishes an in-depth e-mail newsletter providing book reviews, information on author appearances, and other news of interest to book junkies.

Powell's certainly maintains its popularity with Oregonians, just as the Tattered Cover and City Lights bookstores do in Denver and San Francisco, respectively. However, Powell's is far more than a local bookstore. It reaches outside its own state and is known across the country as a mecca for book lovers. For me, no better bookstore exists anywhere.

All the stores chronicled in the pages of this book maintain a fiercely loyal customer base. Powell's is no exception. Customers love this store, so much so that some want to be married there. Over the years the store has played host to several weddings. But the ultimate expression of love is when people choose to spend eternity there. A customer's ashes actually were encapsulated in one of the store's pillars and another's were mixed into the concrete, ultimately becoming part of the floor. Now that is devotion.

CHICAGO ROOTS

In the late 1960s, while a graduate student at the University of Chicago, Oregon-born Michael Powell opened a used bookstore financed with a $3,000 loan from several faculty members. Michael's new business quickly took off. One summer his retired father, Walter, worked in the store and decided he, too, wanted to open a bookstore, in Portland, Oregon, which he did in 1971. Michael joined his dad in the Portland store in 1979, and in 1981 he bought the company from his father and continued to build the business.

Michael Powell tirelessly contributes to the community of Portland and fights with a passion against censorship of any kind. Several of the area's civic groups have honored him for his efforts. He has served on the boards of a number of organizations, including the Multnomah County Library, American Booksellers Association, and Portland Schools Foundation. Every year Powell's makes a substantial donation to the Portland and Beaverton, Oregon, School District to purchase books for its libraries. The store also supports literacy programs, civil rights groups, health education organizations, and local arts organizations. Actively participating in community causes has always played an important role in building a successful retail business. Michael Powell's ongoing dedication to his community and the causes he so vigorously supports has earned him widespread respect. Community involvement also helps the store attract customers.

In 2006, Michael, now in his mid-sixties, took the first steps toward installing new leadership by transferring responsibility for the day-to-day management to his daughter, Emily. Emily previously worked in the online division and in used books and will transition into a leadership role over the next few years. She's a go-getter just like her dad, and soon after moving into her new position she announced a major expansion to the store, including additional floors. The expansion will allow the technical books division, currently housed in a building two blocks away, to be incorporated into the main store. As a truly formidable bookstore already, bringing everything together under one roof can only boost its status as a destination for all types of book lovers.

MICHAEL POWELL'S SECRET TO SUCCESS

Limiting the selection of books available in stores tends to be the strategy major chain bookstores take to build their businesses and maximize sales. Generally they sell highly edited selections of new, bestselling, and backlisted books. Although this strategy works for some booksellers, one disadvantage is that they depend solely on bestsellers to attract customers into their stores. Second, it makes them susceptible to the ever-changing business habits of big publishing companies. And third, booksellers applying this new-book-only strategy limit their ability to distinguish themselves from the competition since they all sell the same books.

Amazon.com takes a different approach, offering a wider selection of books, but online book shopping takes away the pleasure of picking a book up, paging through it, and reading little snippets. While convenient, buying online doesn't compare to the shopping experience in a real bookstore, where one can actually touch the books and spend time browsing the shelves. That's the craving so many book buyers have and shopping online doesn't satisfy it.

Michael Powell recognized early the advantage and profitability of selling used books. By focusing on this area of the book business, Powell's clearly distinguishes itself from the competition and enjoys some healthy profits in the process. As it turns out, when buyers of used books find a reliable and consistent source, they tend to be extremely loyal customers.

Procuring used books for the store and Web site takes great skill and savvy. The staff will buy individual books from people who come through the door every day, but most often they acquire whole collections and merchandise from stores going out of business. Powell's employs some of the best book buyers in the nation and they buy as many as 5,000 used books each day. The staff so effectively buys used books that they now teach other booksellers how to be better at it. Recently Powell's taught the University Book Store staff in Seattle's University District how to improve their used book buying knowledge and skills. This service is available to other booksellers as well.

CREATING A DESTINATION

A retail destination by definition is a place customers will make a special trip to visit. Retailers strive to make their stores a destination. Some succeed; many don't. The goal of creating a very special store for book lovers instead of building a big chain of stores always has been Michael's desire. His absolute focus on the merchandise—new and used books—long ago secured Powell's status as a destination for book enthusiasts.

Most of us who discover the joys of reading do so early on and it grows throughout our lives. The best bookstores understand this and commit to helping readers nurture their love for books. Michael Powell and his staff go above and beyond such a commitment, catering to the broadest needs of book lovers. Long before Starbucks partnered with Barnes & Noble, Powell's had the World Cup Café. This cozy café provides a pleasant gathering place to relax and chat with friends.

Powell's is a destination not only for book lovers in and around Portland but also for visitors to the city from across the country. When guests stay at Portland's leading hotels and request directions to the city's popular tourist attractions, at the top of the list are the Portland Art Museum, the Oregon Museum of Science and Industry, and Powell's City of Books.

POWELL'S AND THE INTERNET REVOLUTION

Using an early Internet bulletin board, Powell's technical division began selling books online in the 1990s. In 1994, more than a year before Amazon.com started, Powell's officially joined the e-commerce revolution, putting its collection of technical books online. Less than two years later the entire inventory of more than one million books became available to Internet shoppers around the world.

Owing to the company's steadfast commitment to used books, selling textbooks to college students became a natural fit. College students, being among the first consumers to embrace the technology, find the Internet to be the most efficient and popular medium to obtain textbooks.

Powell's Internet business operates out of a separate 60,000-square-foot warehouse and is considered among the nation's most distinctive online booksellers. Powells.com sells new, used, and rare books, representing several hundred categories in no less than 130 languages, including Arabic, Chinese, French, German, Hebrew, Italian, Japanese, Korean, Portuguese, Russian, Spanish, and Turkish.

Although Powell's sells new and used books of all types online, rare book sales account for a significant portion of the company's online business. A first edition Lewis and Clark journal sold for $90,000. Also in its rare book collection sit first editions by John Steinbeck, J. R. R. Tolkien, and Laura Ingalls Wilder, and that just scratches the surface. It's interesting to browse the rare books section of Powells .com, even if one's not in the market for a particular title. When looking for out-of-print or hard-to-find books, Powells.com should be first on the list. It continues to prove itself a most reliable resource.

BEST BOOKSTORE IN THE WORLD

Powell's has redefined what a bookstore should be and has earned a reputation unmatched in the book business. It is an exemplary model for independent retailers in any category. I'm not the only one who ranks Powell's among the best stores in America; many others believe it to be the best bookstore in the world.

The *Seattle Times* had this to say: "The greatest bookstore in the world, bar none, sprawls in the blandest of buildings on Portland's Burnside Street." Author Susan Sontag called Powell's "the best bookstore in the English-speaking world." The *Wall Street Journal* refers to Powell's as "one of the most innovative and creative enterprises in the country." Not only celebrities and well-known publications extol Powell's. This store warms the hearts of many book lovers, including an editor working for Portfolio, the publisher of this book. He went to Powell's one day in search of a specific book. He didn't know the title, nor did he know the author's name. He did know it was the book that inspired the movie *Eyes Wide Shut*. When he asked a Powell's associate if she knew of the book, she went to the store's communication system to contact another associate—or so he assumed. Instead, she made a store-wide announcement over the intercom, asking if anyone knew the book on which the movie was based. Five customers took time out from their shopping, made their way to the counter, and spoke with the Portfolio editor. That's the kind of "everyone helps everyone" approach common among employees and customers alike at Powell's.

If you love books, you'll love Powell's City of Books. If you want to see how a true retail superstar does business, Powell's City of Books proves an excellent role model.

POWELL'S CITY OF BOOKS
1005 W. BURNSIDE STREET
PORTLAND, OREGON 97209
(503) 228-4651
WWW.POWELLS.COM

MORE PHOTOS OF POWELL'S CITY OF BOOKS CAN BE SEEN AT
WWW.RETAILSUPERSTARS.COM/POWELLS.

Abt Electronics

The Chicago metropolitan area (also known as "Chicago-land") with the third-largest population in the United States, supports a fiercely competitive consumer electronics and appliance marketplace. Chicagoland consumers can buy these kinds of products from department stores, home centers, drugstores, giant discount stores, warehouse clubs, and hundreds of specialty stores. Add a multitude of on-line merchants and catalogs to the mix, and one can readily see how poor the odds are for a single-location retailer to survive in this environment.

Unlikely? Maybe. Impossible? Not even close. Abt Electronics, a family-run store, beats the odds every day. A favorite destination to find the newest products from the best consumer brands, this store offers Chicago area shoppers far more than selection alone. Abt performs the rarest of feats for a high-volume retailer: extraordinary customer care.

THE PHILOSOPHY

The Abt family's sincere interest in serving customers in ways most unusual these days forms the very core of their approach to business. The atmosphere throughout the store reflects Abt's dedication to customer service. Customers so enjoy the experience that they invariably think of Abt first when they need electronics or appliances. The store's *Customer Service Policy Handbook,* which is only one page, says it all: "The Answer is Always Yes to Any Reasonable Request."

From time to time consumers will take advantage of retailers who use this approach, but the actual number who do is quite small. People appreciate and understand the real value in doing business with this kind of retailer and that's how Abt Electronics continues to thrive.

EXTRAORDINARY CUSTOMER CARE

A typical Abt customer care scenario might involve a couple who needs to replace their old washer and dryer. Having just escaped the obnoxious, used-car-like buy-or-die sales approach at a nearby competitor, they feel a bit apprehensive when the Abt sales associate first greets them. To their relief, he proves himself quite knowledgeable and helpful; such a contrast to the last experience. He knows his stuff and guides them to the models that meet their needs without being pushy. In a painless forty-five minutes, they leave with paperwork in hand and a delivery date scheduled.

While the purchasing process is surprisingly pleasant, the best part of their experience is the delivery. The well-groomed, appropriately dressed, and courteous delivery guys arrive on time and carefully maneuver the new washer and dryer down a narrow flight of stairs into the basement of the couple's home. After completing the installation and cleanup, they thoroughly explain the features of the new washer and dryer and how to use them. That the task of buying major appliances could be so trouble free amazes the couple. Multiply this scenario by thousands of customers, and it's easy to see why Abt enjoys such a loyal following.

A BIT OF HISTORY

"Abt" is the family name, although most Chicagoans refer to the store by its initials—A.B.T. In 1936, Jewel and David Abt opened Abt Radio in the Chicago neighborhood of Logan Square, selling small appliances and radios. As the beginning of a true family venture, Jewel and David ultimately turned over the reins to their son Bob, who went on to open the first Abt Electronics in the Chicago suburb of Niles. Today Bob works closely with his four sons, the third generation in the business of selling electronics and appliances in the Chicago area. Bob is chief executive officer; Michael holds the position of president; Ricky runs customer service, installation, and delivery; Jon handles marketing and Internet; and Billy buys video products and takes care of merchandising.

When regional chains such as Fretter, Highland Electronics, and Polk Brothers began opening superstores in the Chicago market, Bob was forced to take a critical look at the future of his business. Facing increased competition from these larger retailers, he determined it was time to make the move from the small store in Niles to an 80,000-square-foot location a few miles away in Morton Grove. The new facility included an expansive warehouse, 16,000 square feet of retail showroom space, and a parking lot large enough to accommodate the increased traffic.

Adding higher-end electronics and appliances to the merchandise mix helped distinguish the store from the competition. New brands included upscale appliances from Sub-Zero, Miele, and Gaggenau. In the electronics category, high-end audio and home theater systems were added.

In May of 2002, having outgrown the 80,000-square-foot store, Abt Electronics moved into its current home, a massive 350,000-square-foot building on a thirty-seven-acre campus in the suburb of Glenview. The product offerings in this superstore represent more than 150 brands from the world's premier electronics and appliance companies. Today major consumer electronic companies as well as industry media consider Abt Electronics to be the most significant retail enterprise of its kind anywhere in the nation.

When I asked Bob whether or not he had a grand plan for the business, he replied, "Never had a plan. Every time we moved we had been forced to move because we grew out of the place, or new competition was coming to town that probably was going to put us out of business. So it was probably fear." Fear can be a great motivator.

Eventually competitors Fretter, Highland Electronics, Polk Brothers, and Montgomery Ward went out of business, only to be replaced by the country's two largest electronics chains, Best Buy and the now defunct Circuit City. In the last several years such national home center chains as Home Depot and Lowe's, along with regional chain Menards, began selling appliances in their stores. As this is being written, these five companies operate more than sixty stores in the Chicagoland marketplace. While there are differences among them, none offer the selection or level of service that Abt Electronics provides its customers every day.

Abt recently opened a new Design Center building 300 yards south of the main store. "The individual showrooms in the Design Center feature kitchen and bath fixtures, cabinets, lighting, flooring, and more, from companies such as Kohler and Exotic Marble," describes Michael Abt. "The Viking Cooking School (owned by the Viking appliance company) offers a variety of cooking classes, and there's even Jölane's Café & Wine Bar, which offers an extensive variety of food and drink choices throughout the day and evening." Jölane's was named in honor of Jölane "Jewel" Abt, commemorating her many years of dedication to the store and to her family, employees, and customers.

As the Abt family business has grown, so, too, has its appeal to customers around the Midwest. Today Abt's delivery, installation, and service personnel serve the needs of hundreds of customers every day throughout Illinois, Wisconsin, Michigan, and Indiana. Most large appliance, furniture, and electronics retailers outsource delivery, installation, and service these days, resulting in a general deterioration of delivery and service quality. Abt determined early on that it would be advantageous to employ its own staff in this area and maintain its own fleet of trucks and vans. Doing so allows for complete control of the customer experience, from the time a person walks in the door through delivery and installation.

A DIFFERENT WAY TO SERVE CUSTOMERS

A shopping trip to any mall or mass merchant's store reveals the sad state of customer service in American retail. Most often, the only actual interaction one has with another human being takes place at checkout, where cashiers perform the required functions to complete the transaction. Where self-checkout is available, a growing number of shoppers on their own search out what they need and delight in the prospect of eliminating personal contact with that scowling cashier altogether. Frequently the self-checkout lanes at home center stores in most suburban areas of the country have more people waiting in line than the checkouts attended by warm bodies, a.k.a. cashiers.

When making a big purchase, especially one with technical considerations to it, customers prefer human-to-human contact as long as it's with an appropriate expert. At Abt Electronics knowledgeable, amiable salespeople who are available throughout the store willingly and without pressure determine what customers want and need and then skillfully provide information about various products and how product benefits relate to the customer's specific requirements. To top it off, they can even show customers how each product actually works. This is no small feat in such a large store filled with a wide variety of sophisticated and technologically complex electronics. Abt's staff of more than 200 competent, well-trained salespeople gives this store a powerful competitive edge over its big-box neighbors and is one of the reasons customers come back again and again, year after year. And it's not just the salespeople who are friendly and helpful. The cashiers enjoy talking with and getting to know customers as well. A total staff of more than 1,200 dedicated, people-oriented employees keep this store at the top of its game.

NOT THE TYPICAL BIG-BOX STORE

Abt Electronics breaks all stereotypes we've come to expect from big-box stores. They have a tremendous selection of appliances and electronics, which are attractively displayed in tasteful surroundings. Abt successfully uses creative merchandising techniques and props to accentuate their merchandise. The area showing mobile electronics for cars and boats typically features two vehicles and a boat display, fully decked out with complete audio and video systems.

A twenty-foot-long, 7,500-gallon saltwater tropical-fish tank contains no fewer than 100 fish swimming in and around an artificial coral reef. This giant aquarium, modeled after the one at the Mirage Hotel and Casino in Las Vegas, fronts the video camera display providing a visually interesting setting for customers to try out a camera before they buy.

The high-ceilinged atrium, beautifully adorned with flowers, trees, and an impressive marble fountain, provides a focal point around which various boutiques radiate. These stores-within-the-store include The Gourmet Shop displaying small appliances; a high-end kitchen gallery featuring such appliance brands as Sub-Zero,

Viking, Wolf, and Dacor; a fully stocked Sony store; and an Apple Computer boutique. The Home Theater department features full entertainment systems composed of audio and video components as well as specialty furniture to complete the home theater decor. Abt Time Boutique, the newest addition to the atrium, brilliantly displays quality timepieces. This first-class selection of high-end watches appeals to Abt's affluent consumers and perfectly rounds out this area of the store.

The Abt family's obsession with customer care extends to everything with which a customer comes in contact. Often overlooked in retail and a persistent source of consumer ire are unkempt bathrooms. Walking out of nicely merchandised showrooms into dingy, dirty, utilitarian bathrooms can put a damper on anyone's shopping experience and affect their entire opinion of a store. The bathrooms at Abt, designed like those you might find in a five-star hotel, feature marble floors, counters, and subdued lighting. Elegant, comfortable, and always impeccably clean, the bathroom decor adds to the overall shopping experience rather than detracting from it.

CLASSES FOR CUSTOMERS

The salespeople at Abt have done a superb job over the years connecting with customers by helping them make good buying decisions. The store offers another service that creates an even stronger customer bond. Several times each month customers can attend classes on various types of electronics to learn more about and get comfortable with today's sophisticated technologies. Topics such as "How to Use Your Camcorder," "How to Use Your Digital Camera," and "How to Use Your DVD Recorder" help both customers and browsers at every level of technological comprehension get the most from their purchases.

Abt also offers cooking classes covering such topics as "Let's Do Pork," "Knife Skills," and "Hors d'Oeuvres and Appetizers." Taking into account the busy lives of its customers, the store schedules classes both during the day and in the evening. These complimentary, two-hour educational sessions further endear this store to its customers.

THE TRAFFIC

Just how busy the store gets most days fuels the shopping experience at Abt Electronics. Weekends are extremely busy, but the number of people in the store even on weekdays creates a high-energy atmosphere. During four special sales events each year, the number of shoppers increases, raising the excitement level to an all-time high. Three of the sales events focus on existing customers, and the fourth is marketed to the general public. Especially attuned to these sales events, bargain-hunting Chicagoans must exercise patience navigating through the traffic getting into the store and then the traffic within the store itself.

Not long after Abt Electronics moved into its first superstore, it became necessary for traffic police to direct weekend shoppers into and out of the parking lot. It required a lot of circling to get a spot, especially in the years prior to moving into the present location. Wisely, more than 1,000 parking places were allocated for customers at the new facility. Even with that, on a weekend visit to the store to-day, one can expect to find police officers on busy Milwaukee Avenue directing traffic into the lot, where parking places still are at a premium.

While a store with so much traffic might cause some shoppers to go elsewhere, the desire to shop at Abt Electronics rather than a competitor continues to fuel the company's growth. First-time customers may be somewhat frustrated, but ultimately they find the challenge worth it when they experience the selection of items and the extraordinary customer service. Long-time customers know to shop at times when the store is not quite so busy or simply accept that they may have to negotiate their way through lots of traffic to get to the store. When a retailer engenders such fierce customer loyalty, those customers can be quite forgiving when it comes to traffic and even crowds in the store.

TESTING NEW PRODUCTS

Because Abt Electronics is the highest-volume, single-location electronics and appliance retailer in the United States, manufacturers of major brands have found it to be the ideal testing ground for their newest products before making them available to other retailers. One reason for this is the tremendous number of customers who visit the store each week. This allows manufacturers to quickly determine whether the product will be a success in the broader national marketplace. There isn't another store anywhere in the country with as wide a selection of the latest electronics and appliances from the world's preeminent brands.

On any given day one might find the newest high-end audio speakers from Yamaha, cool appliance wizardry from Whirlpool, or the latest high-definition plasma televisions from Pioneer or Panasonic. A paradise for technophiles and lovers of home electronics, Abt Electronics is the place to see products not yet available in any other store in the country.

WEB SITE EXPANDS REACH

True to form, Abt.com reflects the Abt family's commitment to its customers. This easy-to-navigate Web site provides information about the company and the products it sells while making it convenient and secure to buy. It is as much an informational Web site as it is a place to shop.

The site clearly spells out Abt's privacy and shipping policies as well as its Total Satisfaction Guarantee, which allows customers to return an item for a refund within the first thirty days if they are not satisfied. Chicago area customers can also find a calendar of events on the Web site that lists electronics and cooking classes scheduled for the current month.

Among the most popular features on the site are the online buying guides. Guides can be downloaded for every product category, including audio and video equipment, appliances, computer products, and mobile electronics. If a Web site visitor still has questions, Live Chat, available twenty-four hours a day, seven days a week, offers technical assistance as well as customer service help.

The Abt blog contains the latest product and technology news as well as information about upcoming store events and special sales. Photos illustrate special events, products, and anything else that might be of interest to readers. The blog allows the staff at Abt to stay in touch with customers in a more immediate and casual way. With all messages archived, customers can browse past postings or search topics from months past that relate to their current electronic or technological issues or curiosities.

The considerable success of the Web site reflects how much consumers value an easy-to-use site jam-packed with information. Trade publication *Internet Retailer* consistently ranks Abt's Web site among the best on the Internet.

GOING GREEN

Wal-Mart, Home Depot, Whole Earth, and other such national chains embrace environmentally friendly initiatives, but it's not so common for a single-store retailer to take such a comprehensive and costly approach to preserving the environment. Spearheaded by Michael Abt, environmental concerns play an integral role in everything they do to operate the business. The store's giant warehouse, a model of energy efficiency, uses a combination of natural and pulsar lighting, 17 percent more efficient than conventional lighting. The warehouse staff recycles pallets, Styrofoam, and corrugated cardboard. Its power generator uses natural gas and, with its own fleet of delivery and service vehicles, Abt maintains an onsite biofuel refueling station.

"One new project in the works involves the installation of solar panels and a solar windmill on the roof above the store's atrium to generate energy and also serve as an educational display," explains Michael. Additionally the store actively encourages customers to bring in their old TVs and other electronic products for recycling. Abt's new recycling center, located behind the southwest side of its main building, accepts plastics, cardboard, Styrofoam, and old appliances from anyone who wishes to do their part to help the environment.

Abt's environmental initiatives benefit the company in several ways, first and foremost by reducing costs and improving efficiencies. It's simply good business. But working hard to help our environment also affects how the store is perceived in the community. With consumers themselves doing more to protect the environment by recycling and looking for fuel alternatives, a retailer that embraces such initiatives will attract like-minded citizens.

DEFINING SUCCESS

When a retailer truly commits to serving the long-term needs of customers, it doesn't take long for that commitment to be recognized by others. Over the years Abt Electronics has received a great deal of recognition and a number of awards from consumer electronics and appliance industry trade publications, associations, and suppliers. The Better Business Bureau's Torch Award for Marketplace Ethics, bestowed upon Abt in 1998, reflects the Abt family's customer commitment.

The Consumer Electronics Association announced in April of 2008 the induction of the late Jewel and David Abt into the CE Hall of Fame, which "honors leaders whose significant contributions make the consumer electronics industry a vibrant, dynamic, and vital part of our nation and its economy." In July of 2008, *Consumer Reports* named Abt "the best place to shop for major appliances." This honor came as a result of a Consumer Union survey of 20,000 subscribers who voted Abt number one for its wide selection, customer service, and ease of shopping. When pitted against large chain retailers such as Lowe's, Home Depot, and Sears, the selection and service at Abt Electronics rates far superior. Customers and now *Consumer Reports* recognize the difference.

While Abt Electronics has received considerable recognition for its great selection, service, and shopping experience, the Abt family's accomplishments themselves are truly remarkable, especially taking into account the retail segment in which they do business and the fiercely competitive Chicago marketplace. A good number of independent electronics and appliance stores exist around the country, but none have achieved the level of success and consumer adoration as Abt.

Some retailers very publicly make claims of their success. Others quietly go about their business and let their customers define their success. Being a family-owned private enterprise, Abt Electronics isn't obligated to report annual sales the way large, publicly held retail businesses are. Vendors and others familiar with the store approximate annual sales to be in excess of $300 million, with Internet sales alone contributing as much as 10 percent of the total. By any economic measure, this is a very successful retail operation.

Yet, economic measurements tell only part of the story. Equally impressive is the Abt family's penchant for long-term relationships with customers. By one estimate more than 90 percent of the customers coming into the store either have purchased something there before or come in as the result of a referral. Incredible customer loyalty is key to economic success, and it is one reason why Abt Electronics remains unfazed by the multitude of large competitors biting at its heels.

In a category well known for narrow margins and retail failures, Abt Electronics defies the odds and leads the way with innovation and an absolute commitment to its core principles. For anyone even remotely interested in appliances, consumer electronics, and the coolest products for home or automobile, this store is a must-see.

ABT ELECTRONICS
1200 N. MILWAUKEE AVENUE
GLENVIEW, IL 60025
(847) 967-8830
WWW.ABT.COM

MORE PHOTOS OF ABT ELECTRONICS CAN BE SEEN AT
WWW.RETAILSUPERSTARS.COM/ABT.

Zabar's

A sk New Yorkers to list what they miss most when they move away from the city, and more times than not, Zabar's tops the list. America's most populous city, famous for its delicatessens and neighborhood food stores that cater to the city's diverse ethnic groups, upscale consumers, and tourists from around the world, supports more than its share of well-known food emporiums. Dean & DeLuca and Balducci's both have several locations. Newer arrivals in the city include Trader Joe's and Whole Foods. Although foodies seem to be well served, Zabar's remains the one food store loved most by New Yorkers.

It's a rare occasion when Zabar's isn't jammed with shoppers. The store's highly visible location at Eightieth Street and Broadway on the Upper West Side attracts customers from all over the city, not just locals but travelers visiting from around the world. It has to be the most consistently busy store I've ever seen. Describing how busy it is at Zabar's, *Specialty Food Merchandising* magazine said it best: "If you can see the floor, they're having a slow day."

Don't expect an elegantly designed, beautifully merchandised, attractively lit store when visiting Zabar's. It's not that kind of place. But if you are looking for a massive selection of incredible foods to satisfy every taste, people who really know their stuff, and an only-in-New York shopping experience, Zabar's won't disappoint. On one of my visits, I watched an elderly customer having an animated conversation with an employee standing behind the meat counter. She raised her voice and shook her fist at the man, and he yelled back at her. After a few minutes of back and forth, they came to some kind an agreement. She got her package and in a soft, sweet voice turned to him and said, "I'll see you tomorrow."

Zabar's earned its reputation as "New York's finest gourmet food emporium" by offering a broad selection of high-quality foods. The cheese department contains over 600 varieties from Maytag Blue to imported goat's milk to cream cheese. The olive oil selection amazes customers, as do the freshly roasted coffees, smoked fish "to die for," meats, baked sweets, olive breads, and bagels baked to Zabar's specifications offsite, kosher cookies, rugelach, gourmet desserts, dried fruits, imported caviar, homemade soups, and complete meals. The store simply is a gustatory delight. In addition to the vast selection of foods to buy and take home, Zabar's terrific café serves sandwiches, paninis, wraps, blintzes, soups, bagels, smoothies, and more. Lots of stores serve food these days, but Zabar's café serves the same fabulous foods sold in the store.

Coffee ranks among Zabar's many areas of expertise, and the store sells massive amounts. Over the years Saul Zabar has distinguished himself as one of the country's most respected coffee experts. The roasting of the beans is done every Monday to Zabar's extremely critical specifications. When I interviewed Saul in his unpretentious office, he demonstrated his weekly ritual of "cupping" or testing the coffee beans. Even after all these years, Saul tastes and approves all the coffee sold at Zabar's. A video on Zabars.com shows Saul going through the entire process, thoroughly explaining the difference between Zabar's roast and most others.

Although not a technology wonk, Saul has set up his office computer to scroll coffee prices across the screen so he can keep up with current market trends. It's one thing to be a coffee expert, but Saul translates that knowledge and skill into a major part of his store's success, selling as much as 9,000 pounds of roasted coffee beans weekly. By one estimate the store, Web site, and catalog combined sell $2 million to $3 million worth of coffee every year.

YEARS AND YEARS OF CONSISTENT, CAPABLE MANAGEMENT

Zabar's has had just two bosses running the show throughout its seventy-five-year history. Founded in 1934 by Lillian and Louis Zabar, the store sold smoked fish and other such items to its mostly Jewish clientele. Throughout the 1930s and '40s, the business grew and prospered. By 1950 the Zabars had opened five stores. That was the year Louis Zabar died. At the time, their son Saul was a student at the University of Kansas studying medicine with the goal of becoming a doctor. Upon his father's death, Saul left school to take on the responsibilities of running the business along with his brother Stanley for a year, maybe two. He never left.

Saul Zabar, still at the helm at eighty, works no less than forty hours a week, having cut down from his usual sixty to seventy hours in years past. While other merchants try to cut costs by offering lower-quality goods, Saul resolutely carries on his father's policy of selling only superior-quality products. Saul built this extraordinary business as a hands-on owner/manager providing thousands of customers with exactly what they want every single day.

Today Saul, his brother Stanley, his daughter Annie, and several other family members—including children and cousins—work in the business. While many amazing factors ensure this business stands out from the rest, particularly the massive selection, in many ways the store operates just as it has for more than seventy-five years. Employees wear aprons and stand behind counters talking with and serving customers, they stack merchandise as high as possible on counters and shelves, and they show an edgy New York attitude one might expect.

Zabar's takes a highly sophisticated approach to its Internet business, which I find quite impressive. The Web site provides a wealth of information, including a video tour of the store, guide to brewing coffee, recipes, calendar of upcoming events, and an extensive catering menu showing photos of the various foods available for parties. There's a wonderful selection of gift baskets and boxes that combine food products of all sorts. My favorite themed basket has to be the "Zabar's Don't Be Homesick Crate" filled with Zabar's favorites and created for New Yorkers living away from the city. A good percentage of Zabar's regular online and catalog customers are former New Yorkers who remain loyal to the store years after they move away. Web visitors can browse the housewares selection and order everything from bakeware and cutlery to coffee makers and teapots.

THE SELECTION

Saul Zabar has made some important changes to the business as it has evolved over the years. After closing all the other locations except the main store on Eightieth Street and Broadway, he expanded, taking over more and more square footage. Eventually he bought the entire building. Starting in just one small space of less than 2,500 square feet, the store now occupies more than 20,000 square feet on two levels. While Zabar's has long been known as one of the premier food stores in New York City, it may be just as well known among New Yorkers for the vast selection of housewares, gourmet cookware, small appliances, and kitchen gadgets.

The addition of housewares and small appliances can be attributed to Murray Klein, who started out as a stock boy in the early 1950s and eventually became a full partner to Saul and Stanley. The first items sold that didn't fit into a food category were Turkish coffeepots. Without space to display the coffeepots, Murray hung them on hooks from the ceiling. At one time thousands of small appliances and housewares hung from the ceiling of the store. Today you can still find baskets and other small items hanging from the ceiling. Before moving the Housewares Department to the mezzanine level, Zabar's generated an estimated $1 million in revenue just from all that merchandise hanging from the ceiling. Murray Klein retired in 1994 and passed away in 2007.

Today the mezzanine level displays coffeemakers of every kind, including percolators, presses, and espresso/cappuccino/latte makers, as well as teapots, wine refrigerators, fondue sets, more varieties of corkscrews than most customers ever knew existed, blenders, meat grinders, toasters, countertop grills, food processors, rice cookers, waffle irons, pepper mills, thermometers, pots, pans, dishes, cutting boards, peelers, knives, flatware, irons, vacuum cleaners—a total in excess of 25,000 SKUs. Most likely any household item used to prepare food can be found on the mezzanine at Zabar's. Sales from the mezzanine's expansive selection of non-food merchandise contributes significantly to the store's bottom line.

In a city with hundreds of stores selling these same categories of merchandise, two important factors make Zabar's a favorite destination for so many consumers. First, the expansive selection; it's hard to believe so much merchandise can fit in such a small space. The second factor is even more basic—price. Since the very beginning Zabar's has sold merchandise at reasonable prices. Why would anyone shop anywhere else when they can go to Zabar's 365 days a year and buy the same products and brands for substantially less?

AN UNUSUAL APPROACH TO MANAGING PEOPLE

We often hear employers extol the importance of their "family" of employees. Sometimes that's just lip service. Saul Zabar actually treats his employees like part of his family. When employees suffer financial hardships, Saul often lends them money, letting them pay it back a few dollars each week. On one occasion an employee was in need of the tuition to send her disabled son to a boarding school. Saul paid half the tuition. The son now works at Zabar's. By his own estimate, Saul has lent more than $50,000 to employees.

Parking near Zabar's can be quite expensive—if, that is, you can even find a spot. Several years ago Saul acquired a small garage in the neighborhood that he makes available to his employees. Tremendous employee loyalty comes as a result of his largesse, and a good number of the people working at Zabar's have been with the company for two or three decades.

Saul also generously contributes to various organizations within the community. The local Jewish Community Center houses the Saul and Carol Zabar Nursery School dedicated after the Zabars donated $5 million to help build this important addition to the center.

A MIX OF PEOPLE AND CULTURES

The Upper West Side, which is Zabar's neighborhood, has changed demographically over the years. Affluent families living in nearby luxury apartment buildings, young professionals who enjoy the eclectic blend of people and stores, Asian immigrants, and longtime New Yorkers make up the mix today. And they all converge on Zabar's, along with droves of shoppers from outside the neighborhood. By one estimate, Zabar's attracts as many as half its customers from other parts of the city, New Jersey, and Connecticut, not to mention the constant influx of tourists. No wonder the store is always jammed with shoppers.

Crowds of people filling a store to the brim create a palpable energy, a retail phenomenon acknowledged by longtime retailers and other industry observers. This energy often feeds a kind of buying frenzy that can come only from having lots of enthusiastic customers in the store at the same time. Having witnessed this at Zabar's, I can tell you it is certainly fun to watch.

BATTLING THE BIG GUY

A favorite Zabar's story recounts the caviar war waged in the early to middle 1980s between Zabar's and Macy's. Yes, that Macy's—the really big department store with a New York City location covering an entire city block that sponsor's the famous Thanksgiving Day parade. Macy's ran an advertisement during the 1983 Christmas season pricing its highest-grade beluga caviar at $149 a pound. Murray Klein, who then managed the day-to-day operations at Zabar's, countered with $139. Macy's responded with $129, so Zabar's went down to $119.99, which meant selling the caviar at a loss. New Yorkers eagerly anticipated the much publicized annual holiday caviar price war benefiting greatly from the way-below market prices. This war carried on for a few years, until a shortage of caviar precluded Zabar's from continuing the craziness.

BE THE BEST

A wonderful slogan I heard years ago declared, "Be the best, it's the only marketplace that's not crowded." This certainly holds true when describing Zabar's business prowess. This truly incomparable store steadfastly sells only the highest-quality merchandise at reasonable prices. By doing so, the store reportedly generates $50 million in revenue a year.

On one of the online blogs that provide people with the opportunity to critique stores, a customer described Zabar's busy atmosphere as "commotional," but in a good way; that's what makes it so much fun for her. She described the time a little old lady in white gloves and a hat elbowed her to get by, and the day one of Zabar's staff came out from behind the fish counter and pinched her cheeks. And when she couldn't decide what cut of meat she wanted, an "unofficial advisory board at the deli counter" helped out. Where else can you possibly shop and have those kinds of experiences? Zabar's gives customers what they want every day of the year. It is simply the best at what it does.

ZABAR'S
2245 BROADWAY
NEW YORK, NY 10024
(212) 787-2000
WWW.ZABARS.COM

MORE PHOTOS OF ZABAR'S CAN BE SEEN AT
WWW.RETAILSUPERSTARS.COM/ZABARS.

Bronner's Christmas Wonderland

Frankenmuth, Michigan

The quaint central Michigan town of Frankenmuth, with just 5,000 permanent residents, attracts three million tourists each year. Built in the style of a Bavarian village, the community boasts two of the nation's largest family restaurants—Zehnder's and Bavarian Inn—along with cheese and sausage factories, art galleries, museums, and dozens of small shops. But the business that puts Frankenmuth on the map is Bronner's Christmas

Wonderland, the world's largest Christmas store. And it is indeed a wonderland. Residing at 25 Christmas Lane on a forty-five-acre site, this sprawling complex of buildings equals 350,000 square feet covering over seven acres.

Outside throughout the grounds, customers enjoy myriad attractions—a life-size Nativity, the charming Silent Night chapel, dozens of artfully decorated Christmas trees, a seventeen-foot Santa Claus, and a fifteen-foot snowman—all illuminated by more than 100,000 Christmas lights. Bronner's celebrates Christmas all year long, and, if this store had to be described in one word, it would be "festive."

In addition to a dazzling retail showroom, the Bronner's complex houses its shipping department, wholesale division, custom ornament studio, catalog and Internet operations, administrative offices, and warehouse. Additional off-site warehouses hold everything that can't fit in the main warehouse. A massive parking lot surrounding the complex accommodates 1,250 cars and 50 motor coaches.

Shoppers can get a snack in the Season's Eatings Café. Or they can take a break in the Program Center and watch video presentations titled "The World of Bronner's," "A Decorative Life: The Wally Bronner Story," and "Silent Night." Located near the south entrance of the store, the lovely little Silent Night Memorial Chapel, built in 1992, replicates the original Silent Night Memorial Chapel in Obendorf, Austria. The Austrian chapel sits on the site of St. Nicholas Church where "Stille Nacht" ("Silent Night") was first sung on Christmas Eve in 1818. Bronner's Silent Night Memorial Chapel pays tribute to the classic hymn: plaques with the hymn translated into over 300 languages line the walkway to Bronner's chapel. Large snowmen stand on the grounds surrounding the store, along with Santa and his reindeer pulling the sleigh.

The meaning of Christmas will never be lost to commercialism at Bronner's. A great deal of merchandise sold in the store supports the religious aspects of Christmas, and a number of decor items shown both inside and outside promote religious themes. But the most visible recognition of the Bronner family's commitment to the true spirit of the season can be seen in the way the store displays its name, "Bronner's CHRISTmas Wonderland." That very commitment compels many like-minded people to drive great distances to shop at this remarkable store.

FROM SIGN PAINTING TO CHRISTMAS DECORATIONS

While still in high school, founder Wally Bronner began painting signs for local businesses. In 1945, he started a little sign-painting business. He broadened his offerings to accommodate special requests such as decorating parade floats and designing window displays. One day while designing displays for a hardware store in Bay City, Michigan, merchants from nearby Clare commissioned Wally to create Christmas decorations for the town's lampposts. That request was most fortuitous, for commercial Christmas decorations were to become a cornerstone of his business. Like other retailers in this book, the Bronners didn't necessarily have a long-term plan for the business. As more and more customers came to them for Christmas-related products, it became evident this was a pivotal opportunity for growth.

In 1954, Wally and his wife, Irene, moved the business into its first permanent building constructed in the middle of Frankenmuth. The store showcased their commercial Christmas decorations designed for communities and shopping centers. That side of the business took off and today Bronner's is a leading supplier of Christmas decorations for cities and towns, shopping centers and stores, as well as movie sets and television shows.

As the company grew and prospered, Wally and Irene expanded into a former bank building, calling the new store Bronner's Tannenbaum Shop. In addition, they took over a former grocery store, naming it Bronner's Bavarian Corner. With the business spread among three buildings that individually were too small to handle overflow crowds or the inventory needed to serve those customers, it was time to take a big step. In 1977, the Bronners moved their business to the forty-five-acre piece of land in south Frankenmuth where it resides today. In the late 1970s, Wally and Irene sold the sign-making business and devoted all their attention to Christmas decorations.

Today Wally and Irene's children run the business, with Wayne Bronner as president and chief executive officer, Maria Bronner Sutorik and Carla Bronner Speltzer serving as vice presidents, and each of their spouses managing key areas in the store. More than fifty years after its founding, Bronner's Christmas Wonderland continues to be a true family business.

LIKE NO OTHER STORE IN THE WORLD

Most Americans are familiar with Christmas displays in department stores and perhaps have visited one of the many small stores around the country specializing in Christmas merchandise. Using these stores as a point of reference makes it difficult to describe the breadth of merchandise offered in the Bronner's 98,000-square-foot showroom. Festive holiday merchandise and displays surround visitors with every step they take through the store. Everywhere one looks, colorful decorations, gifts, trees, and other Christmas-related goods (many manufactured specifically for Bronner's) fill the store from floor to ceiling.

Customers can choose from more than 6,000 ornaments, 50,000 trims, thousands of light sets, 150 nutcrackers, Santa suits and hats in every size, outdoor decorations, dishes and glassware, a great selection of German steins, stockings to hang on the mantle, Advent calendars, Christmas cards, music CDs, books, artificial trees, and thousands of gift items, including toys and teddy bears for children. Among the most popular items are personalized ornaments and stockings for the entire family. Three hundred and fifty fully decorated trees of every size, shape, needle type, and color one can imagine are on display year-round. Bronner's uses various motifs when decorating the trees, such as religious, traditional, and toy-land. Customers enjoy the wide variety and can get ideas for decorating their own trees.

Limited-edition ornaments as well as a wide selection of Department 56 and Precious Moments figurines make up some of the collectibles available for purchase. And in keeping with the true meaning of Christmas, the book department stocks a fine selection of bibles in twenty languages.

As an important part of the Christmas celebration, Nativity scenes play a major role at Bronner's. Customers can choose from small sets that will fit in the palm of the hand to grand life-size depictions of Jesus Christ's birth. An impressive 570 Nativity scenes from sixty-five countries comprise the Bronner family's permanent collection. And Nativity ornaments hang from every one of the 350 decorated Christmas trees.

In 1974, the Bronner's artisans began customizing and dating glass ornaments that customers could treasure as keepsakes for years to come. Shoppers can now choose from 200 hand-personalized Christmas ornaments expertly crafted by one of the many talented artists on staff. Personalized ornaments have become one of Bronner's most popular offerings. Customers from across the country come back for new ornaments year after year.

This being the world's largest Christmas store and the world's largest seller of Christmas merchandise, Bronner's must tap the resources of suppliers all over the world. To acquire the wide variety of ornaments and other Christmas-oriented products, the company's buyers bring in merchandise from vendors in thirty countries, representing six continents.

CHRISTMAS—BIG BUSINESS AT BRONNER'S

In most stores Christmas is a seasonal business. At Bronner's it's the only business. The retail store, as the best-known and most visible part of the business, attracts hundreds of thousands of customers to Frankenmuth each year. But that's not all there is to the Bronner family's Christmas business.

Bronner's retail catalog has grown from an eight-page flyer into sixty-plus slick, full-color pages mailed to two million customers yearly. Its Internet business started in 1997 with just 100 items. Today the Web site displays more than 5,000 items. That's only the retail side. Bronner's enjoys a substantial wholesale business as well, supported by its own catalog and wholesale Web site. Resellers can choose from approximately 3,000 items not available to them anywhere else.

The newest addition to Bronner's online presence—MyChristmas Wonderland.com—allows visitors to view Christmas lights displays using a variety of search options from Google Maps. Customers can search for local displays that they can visit personally or they can virtually visit decorated homes around the world. People who create Christmas lights displays place their addresses and post photos of their home displays on the site. In addition to making the Bronner's Web site even more popular with consumers, it allows people to find the best home Christmas displays in their own communities.

A BIG STORE NEEDS LOTS OF PEOPLE

Being open 361 days a year and a peak traffic season lasting from June through December, Bronner's requires a substantial team on board. During the peak season, the staff grows to upward of 600 team members, including managers and supervisors. As it is with all great places to work and with many of the stores in this book, staff longevity is common at Bronner's. Seniority among managers and supervisors averages twenty-plus years, and a significant number of temporary team members come back to work the peak season year after year.

When I visited Bronner's Christmas Wonderland, I arrived early for my appointment with Wayne Bronner, allowing me to spend an hour or so wandering around the store before my formal tour. The folks at the reception desk greeted me and genuinely made me feel welcome. As I walked through the store, I had the opportunity to talk with several team members, all of whom were friendly, helpful, and attentive.

It didn't take long to find several items I wanted to buy. In a high-volume store such as this, one might expect to wait in line to pay for purchases. But with more than enough registers open, my checkout was quick and efficient. While the cashier rang up my sale, another team member individually boxed my items to ensure they remained intact for my travel home.

I love to visit stores with terrific displays and great merchandise, but I am a stickler for customer service. I most enjoy shopping where the staff is friendly and attentive, and genuinely cares whether I have a pleasant shopping experience. The Bronner's staff did everything to meet and exceed my expectations.

BUILDING THE BUSINESS

When asked whether he had a plan for growth, Wayne Bronner replied, "No, we haven't had anything like a grand plan for the business." Every one of the businesses in this book was built and has sustained its growth with an absolute focus on the customer. Repeat customers and word-of-mouth advertising fuel the growth of each of these businesses. On a single day, more than 26,000 people came through the doors of Bronner's. This does not happen unless lots of happy customers tell lots of other people about the store.

In addition to strong referrals from satisfied customers, the store has been featured on NBC's *Today* show, *CBS This Morning,* ABC's *Good Morning America* and *The Home Show,* the Travel Channel, and many more television shows and movies. Bronner's advertises in dozens of newspapers and magazines and tells its story on sixty billboards spread across the country. A diverse array of special events attracts customers to the store as well. Annual Precious Moments and Department 56 promotions draw collectors from all over. Fine artists do ornament signings and glassblowing. And, of course, kids always love Santa's regular appearances in December as well as the Easter Bunny's each spring.

Prior to his death in 2008, Wally Bronner liked to tell stories of families that came to the store year after year. He often saw customers who first came to the store as young married couples and continued to shop with their children, grandchildren, and even great-grandchildren. It is not uncommon for four generations of one family to shop Bronner's for Christmas decorations and gifts.

THE IMPORTANCE OF BEING
THE BIGGEST AND THE BEST

The Bronner family continues to expand and leverage its position as the world's leader in Christmas merchandise, even as the nation's mass merchants broaden their selections. The company's success directly results from its commitment to dominating the category. Stocking unique and interesting merchandise and exceeding customer expectations will keep Bronner's at the top. Getting past Wal-Mart to become the world's largest at anything is considered unfathomable, but plenty of retail specialties are yet to be dominated by any one retailer.

By dominating the Christmas business, Bronner's proves that being a remarkable retailer means more than having a big store. Remarkable means creating a true destination and being top-notch at every aspect of the business. Delighting and dazzling shoppers with unique merchandise and excellent service gives customers compelling reasons to come back again and again. While some retailers may be fixated on opening new stores, the folks at Bronner's spend all their time making their one store, Web site, and catalog the best.

Retail success requires satisfying legions of customers, and Bronner's Christmas Wonderland does this extraordinarily well. One of retail's most effective competitive strategies is to create a business that cannot be duplicated. By every measure Bronner's Christmas Wonderland has done just that.

BRONNER'S CHRISTMAS WONDERLAND

25 CHRISTMAS LANE

FRANKENMUTH, MI 48734

(989) 652-9931

WWW.BRONNERS.COM

MORE PHOTOS OF BRONNER'S CHRISTMAS WONDERLAND CAN BE SEEN AT WWW.RETAILSUPERSTARS.COM/BRONNERS.

Ron Jon Surf Shop

Cocoa Beach, Florida

The sport of surfing first gained notice after World War II but became all the rage with the popularity of the 1960s beach movies. Surfing today is as much a lifestyle as it is a sport and enthusiasts travel all over the world to ride and experience the oceans' waves. According to a recent *New York Times* article, more than 2.7 million Americans consider themselves surfers. And even more have adopted the surfer lifestyle.

Surf shops have sprung up from Florida to Hawaii serving the needs of everyone from hard-core surfers to surfer wannabes and others who simply like to wear surf-oriented apparel. In Southern California, where surfing is a part of daily life for locals and tourists alike, literally dozens of surf shops line the streets of beach communities, from San Luis Obispo to the Mexican border. To satisfy the needs of consumers, general merchandise stores such as Target and Costco stock surf-related merchandise as well.

Surf shops even do well in Midwest cities such as Chicago, Kansas City, and Cleveland. Several years ago Abercrombie & Fitch dove in, so to speak, and opened surf-oriented stores called Hollister. Designed to look like a beach house on the California coast, Hollister sells beach- and surf-wear to young consumers. Although enjoying spectacular growth, these mall-based stores aren't what those in the surfer subculture call "real" surf shops.

The one indisputably authentic surf shop known worldwide as the biggest and best is Ron Jon Surf Shop in Cocoa Beach, Florida.

IT ALL STARTED WITH A SURFBOARD

In 1959 when young Ron DiMenna wanted to buy a custom-made surfboard from California, his father recommended, "Buy three, sell two at a profit, then yours will be free." Not long after that, Ron Jon Surf Shop opened on Long Beach Island, New Jersey. Yes, the Ron Jon empire began as a tiny shop on the Jersey shore in 1961. Two years later Ron opened his first Florida surf shop, measuring just 1,000 square feet at the end of Canaveral Pier on the east coast of Florida. With a casual atmosphere and merchandise displayed on crates, the shop proved to be the perfect surfer hangout. From this inauspicious start grew the world's best-known and most successful surf shop.

Ron Jon in Cocoa Beach, more than forty years old and by far the largest surf store anywhere, attracts almost two million visitors annually. In recent years Ron Jon has opened several more stores in

Florida as well as in Orange, California; Myrtle Beach, South Carolina; and even licensed shops in Canada; Cozumel, Mexico; and Grand Turk on the Turks and Caicos Islands. While the others are fine stores, none compare to the flagship Ron Jon Surf Shop in Cocoa Beach. It is a one-of-a-kind store providing a one-of-a-kind shopping experience.

A TRUE ONE-OF-A-KIND STORE

The block-long Cocoa Beach store stands out from other architecturally interesting buildings detailed in this book because of its bold colors, dramatic facade of large windows, captivating statuary, and rotating billboard. Being situated on A1A, one of the busiest highways in Florida, allows for easy access and great visibility. The Cocoa Beach store undergoes a face-lift every few years as the design team experiments with various attention-grabbing color combinations. For a period of time it was an eye-catching teal and pink. The store now sports a bold blue intricately trimmed in shades of yellow and orange characteristic of the art deco style. On the plaza that fronts the store stands artfully detailed, bigger-than-life sand sculptures of a surfer, skateboarders, and beach volleyball players.

At 52,000 square feet, Ron Jon offers a tremendous selection of artfully displayed apparel, surf gear, and board-sports-related equipment. The assortment of boards alone—from small body and skim boards to longer six-foot-plus surfboards—staggers the senses. Accessories include countless varieties of board bags, fins, wax, wet suits, and other surf gear and apparel.

Among the hottest items in board stores these days are skateboards and accessories. Ron Jon carries a serious assortment of skateboard decks, complete skateboards, and inline action boards in a medley of shapes, sizes, and colors, including some sporting the Ron Jon logo. At Ron Jon, skateboarders will not be disappointed.

While offering a wide range of apparel for men, women, and children on two floors, Ron Jon may be best known for its massive

T-shirt selection. At last estimate 350,000 T-shirts were being sold each year. Its constantly changing selection of forty-two designs in every style and color imaginable allows few customers to walk out without buying several for themselves as well as family and friends. The store offers a mega selection of caps as well. For the person who needs to carry a bottle-opener with him at all times, Ron Jon sells a cap with a bottle-opener built right into the bill—one of those must-have items. Of course, the basic low-profile Ron Jon cap can be worn almost anywhere anytime.

A number of brands dominate the surf market these days, as is the case within other specialty categories. Ron Jon's choices of Billabong, Hurley, Oakley, O'Neill, Quiksilver, Rip Curl, Roxy, Rusty, and Volcom merchandise rank second to none. In addition to the large assortment of these best-known surf and beachwear brands, Ron Jon offers a broad array of merchandise under its own brand, adding to this store's strengths. Leveraging its well-established and respected brand, Ron Jon offers a wide selection of logoed merchandise.

Shoppers find the breadth of goods available at this Cocoa Beach treasure alluring. Not only does Ron Jon carry apparel and surf equipment, it also has a wide selection of surf-related household and home decor items, including glassware, doormats, rugs, mirrors, and frames, as well as items for the bed, bath, and kitchen. Surfers who want their homes to accurately reflect their interests can buy surfboard-shaped area rugs in both four- and six-foot sizes.

MARKETING WITH BILLBOARDS

Some so-called marketing experts advise against using billboards to market a store. They feel retailers would be better off spending their marketing dollars on mass media—radio, TV, and newspapers. These same experts will tell retailers that if they are really savvy, they will employ Web sites such as Myspace.com and Facebook.com to spur word of mouth from customers. But Ron Jon very successfully uses billboards to attract attention and bring customers to the store, and it has done so for a very long time.

Ron Jon's billboards can be seen throughout Florida. Claiming an estimated 500 million consumer impressions annually, it's virtually impossible to miss one while traveling the state's highways. The abundance of billboards brought about the Ron Jon billboard game where travelers try to guess how many miles they will have to drive before seeing the next Ron Jon billboard. The game has done a nice job of distracting and entertaining children for years. One of the great things about building a retail business is the variety of methods retailers can employ to attract customers. For Ron Jon billboards work very well, as is attested by its nearly two million visitors every year.

Billboards remain the store's primary marketing vehicle, but they are not the only medium used to attract visitors. Ron Jon's television advertising targets tourists and residents alike, and its print ads appear in multiple tourist-oriented publications. International shoppers find this surf mecca to be as fabulous as do Americans. Tourists from more than fifty countries visit yearly.

This highly entertaining, tourist-oriented retail store literally attracts busloads of shoppers. Each year approximately 1,000 busses filled with surfers, beach lovers, sun worshippers, and vacationers show up at Ron Jon. Certainly carloads of shoppers pulling into a retailer's parking lot would please any store owner, but it is a retailer's dream to see busses filled with people pull up to the store and unload shoppers who then clamor inside. Upon exiting, they're carrying bags and bags practically overflowing with merchandise. At Ron Jon it happens with great regularity. Being located not far from Orlando and near the Kennedy Space Center certainly helps, but Ron Jon Surf Shop is a great attraction all on its own.

SPECIAL EVENTS

Multiple special events held at Ron Jon every year play a big part in attracting visitors. Live bands play most Saturday and Sunday afternoons throughout the summer months, making the store a popular destination for music lovers as well as surf-shop fans. The store brings in musical groups of all kinds, from school marching bands to rock bands.

The "Show Us Your Ron Jon T-Shirt Contest" takes place every summer in Cocoa Beach where Ron Jon fans send in photos of themselves wearing Ron Jon T-shirts in exotic locations. A staggering number of those 350,000 T-shirts sold every year turn up in places one would never expect to see them. Customers take it as a challenge to come up with new and unusual places to wear their T-shirts. The number of entries in this contest increases from year to year and the judges get a kick out of the creative photography sent in by T-shirt–wearing travelers.

The Billabong Girls Surf Camp comes to Shepard Park behind the store every August and is specifically geared toward women and girls eight years old and up. Appearances by the world's best-known surfers as well as book signings take place at Ron Jon throughout the year. Recently the store hosted the Roxy Model Search and Fashion Show, which helped select the next spokesmodel for the surf-oriented Roxy brand.

The biggest event of all—the Annual Ron Jon Easter Surf Festival—just celebrated its forty-fifth anniversary. During this four-day event, Ron Jon hosts more than 300 surfers of all ages. The festival, composed of professional and amateur surf competitions, autograph signings, and lots of live music and entertainment, draws thousands of visitors to Cocoa Beach, most of whom spend a good deal of time in the store.

A TRAVELING MAN

More than twenty years ago Ron DiMenna left the day-to-day operations of the business to others and began traveling with his wife, Lynne. He outfitted a forty-three-foot-long motor coach with as much electronic wizardry as he would need to keep in touch with the business and travel in style. But it's the outside of his current motor coach that attracts the most attention. Colorfully designed, it resembles an old Woody station wagon with a large Ron Jon logo on the back and surfers riding a wave painted on both sides. As the DiMennas travel the countryside, Ron Jon coach sightings thrill people, who eagerly snap pictures of this unique vehicle.

Ron DiMenna still owns the business, but today it is ably managed by President Debbie Harvey, a former department store executive.

THE POWER OF THE BRAND

When talking about the power of a brand, consumer products companies such as Coca-Cola, Budweiser, and Kleenex come to mind. Although Gap, Wal-Mart, and Target might also be considered, smaller retailers rarely are. From day one the Ron Jon management took great care to nurture and leverage the Ron Jon brand. By doing so they have succeeded in establishing Ron Jon among the top iconic surf and lifestyle brands.

With the great popularity of stickers, Ron Jon has found that colorful stickers effectively promote the store and brand. Every customer who buys something gets a free sticker with Ron Jon's famous logo. Those stickers subsequently have turned up in extraordinary places, including the MIR space station, the Eiffel Tower, and the bumpers of cars around the world. The stickers, along with all the globe-traversing T-shirt wearers, give Ron Jon's logo massive exposure.

In 2002 the Chrysler Corporation provided a most innovative extension of the Ron Jon brand, the introduction of the special edition Ron Jon PT Cruiser. The Ron Jon PT Cruiser, decked out with Ron Jon graphics on the hood and side panels, came with beach accessories such as a beach blanket, towel, and T-shirt. The Ron Jon PT Cruiser package became a very hot item, with only a limited number available exclusively to Florida residents.

The Ron Jon retail enterprise continues to grow, opening new stores, licensing its brand around the world, and enjoying ongoing success. Meanwhile the flagship store maintains its individuality and reaps the benefits of Ron Jon's brand recognition. Anyone charged with building a retail brand would do well to use Ron Jon Surf Shop as a role model. It holds an enviable position.

RON JON SURF SHOP

4151 N. ATLANTIC AVENUE

COCOA BEACH, FLORIDA 32931

(321) 799-8888

WWW.RONJONS.COM

MORE PHOTOS OF RON JON SURF SHOP CAN BE SEEN AT
WWW.RETAILSUPERSTARS.COM/RONJONS.

A Southern Season

Michael Barefoot, owner and founder of this legendary food emporium, came into the food business in a
rather roundabout way. As is the case with all the stores
profiled in this book, A Southern Season sets its own standards and follows its own management style, often challenging retail traditions.

WHY FOOD? WHY NOT?

For generations young adults, when faced with real-world career decisions, have struggled to "find" themselves. Michael Barefoot was no exception. He had no idea what to do with his life. What did he want as his career? All through his university years he kept looking, trying one career path after another, but nothing seemed to fit. He knew there was a niche out there for him—he just had to find it.

He looked deep within himself, asking, "What is interesting to me? What do I not get tired of?" He knew his heart never wavered from the world of food. "I went out and lied my way into every kind of job in the country in the food business," he recalls. "Country clubs and distributorships and manufacturing operations, retail, wholesale, everything I could dream of in the food world just to get a glimpse of what was out there." But he still couldn't find anything he thought he could make his career.

In 1975, armed with insight and a great deal of determination, he opened an 800-square-foot store in Chapel Hill, North Carolina. "I chose Chapel Hill because we opened that store on something much shorter than a shoestring." Not having money for advertising, which would be a requisite in a larger city, he reasoned, "Chapel Hill was small, it was sophisticated, but it seemed to be a place where word of mouth could be my advertising."

He roasted coffee beans and sold hard-to-find foods, which in those days included items common in today's grocery stores, such as wine vinegar and capers. The concept of a fancy foods store didn't really exist in 1975, and it took considerable efforts to acquire that which he chose to sell. Prior to opening his store, Michael had worked for a year in a Winston-Salem grocery store that carried some specialty foods. He developed a few contacts from that experience, but they were just a fraction of what he would need to fully merchandise his new store. He proceeded to write hundreds of letters to governments and consulates around the world in order to identify suppliers for the foods he wanted to offer.

He learned quickly that he had to do more than sell food. The people coming in the door and returning over and over again weren't there solely because of the food. Michael explains his philosophy. "I think there's something special about the food world that's very intimate. We're certainly in the food business, but there's a whole other level that's not about food at all. It's about human interaction. We're here to make people feel better when they leave than when they came in." This is accomplished with a warm and comfortable shopping environment and by providing every customer with a pleasant shopping experience.

By 1978, the store had outgrown its 800 square feet and relocated to a larger space. They moved again in 1992, and the latest incarnation, a beautifully renovated brick building and the most prominent feature at Chapel Hill's University Mall, opened in 2003. Now occupying 59,000 square feet on two levels, this attractively appointed food store offers more than 75,000 items. Among its many strengths are the breadth and quality of the international gourmet foods, wines, housewares, and cookware, as well as goods from its own state of North Carolina.

Today, gourmet and fancy foods stores are intrinsic to the retail environment all across the country, but none better exemplifies what one wants and expects from this type of store better than A Southern Season.

WHAT MAKES IT SPECIAL

Gourmet foods attract a more discerning customer than that of the general grocery shopping public. Those people with a taste for the gourmet expect a high level of service provided by a knowledgeable sales staff. The people working at A Southern Season are not only some of the most knowledgeable but also the most cordial you will find anywhere. The staff of 250 exemplifies Southern charm, gentility, and grace. But great customer service goes beyond being friendly and attentive. It entails policies, procedures, and systems that place the customer at the center of every consideration and decision.

I found one policy quite unusual and absolutely geared toward customer convenience. A Southern Season opens five minutes before the posted opening time and closes no less than five minutes after. Michael says of this policy, "Out there somebody's watch is wrong and he's going to be inconvenienced and unhappy." Closing time frequently extends beyond the five extra minutes to accommodate customer needs.

How many times have you gone to a store, only to stand outside waiting for the prescribed opening time while the store's associates stand around drinking coffee and chatting with each other? And how often have you been rushed to make a purchase because it's closing time and the manager or owner is trying to relieve the staff so as to not keep them on the clock longer than absolutely necessary? When customers hold the true focus of the business, these things do not happen.

In the early days, the small coffee roastery needed to generate $312 a day in sales to keep the doors open. On days when the sales number wasn't achieved, Michael would stay open until he hit the number. Sometimes that meant staying open until midnight. This is an important lesson, particularly for anyone starting out in business. By paying absolute attention to what it costs to operate the business every day, retailers just starting out can make sure they generate enough revenue to keep the doors open until gaining some sales momentum.

A TOUR OF A SOUTHERN SEASON

The aroma of freshly brewed coffee coming from the large Coffee and Tea Department envelops customers as they walk through the doors. Customers can sample from the several featured coffees and teas offered that day. With its roots in the coffee business, the store accommodates coffee aficionados looking for the world's best ground or whole-bean coffees. The tantalizing aroma of fresh coffee alone will bring you back.

Customers can sample foods throughout the store as well. Michael believes that's what it's all about. "If I can put something in your mouth that you love the taste of, you'll buy it." Walking down the left side of the store, shoppers can sample anything that intrigues them from the Bakery, Cheese Department, Salad Bar, Prepared Foods, or Deli. Along with foods from outside resources, the store's own kitchen concocts a full range of food and deli choices daily.

Farther down the left side, beyond the Deli, the Candy and Confection Department presents a tempting array of imported chocolates, Jelly Belly brand jelly beans in a multitude of flavors, and other candies that should satisfy the sweetest sweet tooth. Chocolate-dipped fruits and nuts as well as the finest Belgium chocolates, all available for sampling, make this a heaven on earth for chocoholics.

Cookware, knives, accessories, glassware, cookbooks, seasonal merchandise, and a selection of beautiful Vietri ceramics from Italy are found in the House and Home Department located in the center of the store. Just beyond House and Home is Center Stage, a sampling area. While sampling takes place throughout the store, Center Stage features special items. Demonstrations and tastings take place there on most weekends. The "What's in Store" section of Southernseason.com lists upcoming events. A Fourth of July special titled "Fun Foods" featured potato salad, fried chicken, and red, white, and blue trifle. Tips, tastings, and recipes for picnics were presented. Another weekend, "We All Scream for Homemade Ice Cream" demonstrated how easy it is to make ice cream in the Cuisinart ice cream maker.

Circling around to the rear right of the store, one encounters over 2,000 varieties of quality domestic and imported wines, ranging from moderately priced bottles to some of those "Wait-That-Bottle-Can't-Possibly-Cost-That-Much" vintages. Regular social events revolve around this diverse selection of wines. "Fridays Uncorked" and "Saturday Wine Nights" rank high on Chapel Hill's popular weekend activities. Music is always a part of these events as well, making "Fridays Uncorked" and "Saturday Wine Nights" about 50 percent social and 50 percent wine. No formal presentations are made, so people can drop in whenever they want. Wine themes are designated for the evening and wine pros serve as resources with books in hand, ready to talk. If someone has questions or wants to discuss wine, the wine pros talk to them one on one. People go to the store's wine events on dates or drop by on their way to a movie or out to dinner. Michael notes, "In the process, they go home with some wine they've discovered they love. Smiles, always smiles, walking out the door."

On this side of the store customers can choose from a large selection of imported and domestic packaged foods, spices, and seasonings, as well as items from its significant Gift Basket Department. The Floral Department may be one of the finest you will find outside a florist's shop. A spacious, nicely laid out checkout makes it easy for customers to complete their purchases.

The Weathervane Restaurant in A Southern Season measures 6,500 square feet and can handle large groups for special events. The friendly staff serves breakfast, lunch, and dinner daily. The menus offer dishes to satisfy a variety of preferences along with some unique selections, such as Shrimp and Grits and Bacon, Lettuce, and Fried Green Tomato Sandwiches. In casual dining restaurants, which have proliferated in recent years, the decor often runs from very simple to tacky. Not so at the Weathervane; it might best be described as casual elegance. The decor is comfortable and classy without being pretentious.

COOKING SCHOOL AND SPECIAL EVENTS

Culinary Lessons at A Southern Season (C.L.A.S.S.) are conducted in a state-of-the-art facility upstairs from the main floor of the store. In-house staff as well as famous guest chefs and wine experts teach more than 250 classes annually. Large overhead mirrors and television monitors for class participants enhance the fifty-seat, stadium-style viewing area. An additional outdoor classroom and grill allow the school to conduct two classes simultaneously.

Unlike cooking schools that use commercial appliances, C.L.A.S.S. uses Sub-Zero and Wolf appliances, much like what the students use in their own homes. Classes cover such topics as New Orleans classics, exotic Asian dishes, seafood, cakes and cookies, and just about any other dish one may want to master. Regular book signings from well-known chefs and food writers add to the prestige of the school.

In addition to its extremely popular cooking school and weekend tastings, A Southern Season holds special food events throughout the year. In the spring, the annual Festival of Women celebrates and honors the accomplishments of women in the specialty food and gift industries. Lots of cooking classes, representatives from food companies, along with demonstration and sampling stations throughout the store, contribute to the success of this event. The proceeds from ticket sales benefit local charities.

The North Carolina Food and Wine Fest, an annual fall event at the store, lasts five days and features foods and wines produced in-state. The store's event coincides with Taste of the State, a daylong event held in the parking lot of the local mall.

It's only natural that A Southern Season would seek out other ways to educate and teach its customers in addition to its cooking school, Web site, and monthly e-mail newsletter that provides recipes and insights into gourmet foods. To that end, *Side Dish* airs weekly on WCHL, a local radio station. The show, hosted by A Southern Season's own Deborah Miller and Jay White, can be heard each Sunday, with a repeat broadcast the following Saturday.

THE BIG, ONCE-A-YEAR SALE

The state of North Carolina was once among those states that at the end of the fiscal year assessed a property tax on retail inventory. A Southern Season's fiscal year ended June 30. Being a college town, when school recessed for the summer, Chapel Hill emptied out. Business was the slowest during June, July, and August for the entire community. It made sense to sell down the inventory at the end of the fiscal year, reducing the tax liability, and restocking fresh for when school resumed in the fall. Starting the very first year in business, A Southern Season drastically marked down prices and held an inventory reduction sale that lasted the whole month of June, resulting in its being the second busiest month of the year.

Most states no longer assess annual inventory taxes, but the annual sale at A Southern Season has taken on a life of its own. The sale attracts shoppers countrywide. Bargain hunters arrive in every kind of vehicle—from Winnebagos for camping out in the parking lot to cars towing trailers. "It brings out the worst in people," Michael laughs. "When that sale starts, perfectly well-behaved, dignified customers steal things from each other's carts. We have police in the parking lot." Store sales certainly are nothing new, but generally retailers hold too many sales to make them special. Promoting just one sale a year makes it an event.

A TRUE MULTICHANNEL BUSINESS

Single-location retailers tend to make their physical store their entire focus. Not so at A Southern Season. The first extension outside the store was into the catalog business. Much of the merchandise available in the store is also illustrated in the catalog, along with a comprehensive gift basket selection. The gift baskets target individual consumers as well as corporate accounts. Christmas gifts in a recent holiday catalog ranged in price from under $10 for modest gifting all the way up to $295 for elegantly presented gift baskets featuring gourmet delicacies and fine wine.

Today A Southern Season operates an 80,000-square-foot distribution center in Hillsborough, North Carolina. This facility serves as the fulfillment location for both its catalog and growing Internet business. It also houses a call center and handles distribution for Carolina Cupboard, the company's wholesale division.

UNCONVENTIONAL MANAGEMENT STRUCTURE

Not long after Michael opened his original store, he hired his first employee. Unschooled in traditional management techniques and not knowing how to delegate, he took a piece of chalk, drew a line down the middle of the store, and said, "Okay this is my half. In my half I do everything. I mop the floor at night, I order the merchandise, I stock the shelves, I sell things, and I write checks for the bills. That's your half. Do the same over there."

The management structure at A Southern Season differs little today from when the first store opened. The people who run each of the departments rose from within; Michael doesn't even look outside to find managers. He says they're really good at "growing" their own people. Once they move into a department manager position, they rarely leave because they love what they do. Each of the eight departments— Candy and Confection; Coffee; Floral and Gift; Gourmet Grocery; House and Home; Prepared Food, Deli, Cheese, and Bakery; Weathervane; and Wine—is managed as an individual store semi-autonomously, with its own mini profit and loss statements.

The managers' jobs are to run their departments as though they were a sole proprietorship. While success or failure rests on their shoulders, they don't have to take any of the risks of owning their own businesses. These "merchants" do their own buying of the merchandise and determine the price at which it's sold. They hire whomever they want, pay them whatever they want, and train them however they want. Once a year they all meet to make their sales projections and plan for the coming year. Once a week the merchants get together to share ideas, discuss challenges, fine-tune their plans, and socialize. Michael gets great joy from watching them succeed.

This approach to managing a specialty food store puts the equivalent of a collection of individual stores under the same roof, much like a mall, with a common set of objectives. This unusual strategy of allowing individual merchants to completely manage all of the functions of their own areas within the store has worked well for A

Southern Season. The store has seen consistent growth for over thirty years, with sales estimated at more than $30 million annually.

A VISUAL AND GUSTATORY DELIGHT

In 2004 Michael Barefoot and his store were honored by the National Association for the Specialty Food Trade as its Outstanding Retailer of the Year. That same year, *Gourmet News* bestowed its Retail Achievement Award upon A Southern Season for its work in the area of food education. It has been featured in *Travel + Leisure* magazine, *Southern Living* magazine, *Gourmet Retailer,* and on the Food Network. Food media recognition surely contributes to a store's celebrity, but happy customers make the best ambassadors. Customers delight in telling Michael the unusual places they've seen the Southern Season name, the most exotic of which was a logoed shopping bag spotted in Tokyo, Japan.

A significant trend in retailing points to the importance of entertaining consumers. Michael Barefoot and his staff not only sustain an entertaining retail environment, hosting special events every week, but they also provide a superb shopping and food education experience. Unlike stores with entertainment features such as those found in Jungle Jim's International Market, A Southern Season should not be considered a store with a "shoppertainment" approach to the business. Entertaining customers here is more about frequent special events, the store's sampling program, and its cooking school, which bring about a pleasant social experience and feeling about the store itself. This single store attracts gourmet food and fine wine lovers from all over the United States.

The late *New York Times* food critic Craig Claiborne once described A Southern Season as "wall to wall and floor to ceiling . . . a visual and gustatory delight!" I couldn't agree more!

A Southern Season
201 S. Estes Drive
Chapel Hill, North Carolina 27514
(919) 929-7133
www.southernseason.com

More photos of A Southern Season can be seen at
www.retailsuperstars.com/southernseason.

ABC Carpet & Home

New York,
New York

As North America's largest consumer marketplace, New York City plays host to plenty of stores selling home furnishings. But ABC Carpet & Home, widely recognized for its exquisite design and almost magical beauty, serves up seven floors of distinctive merchandise imported from around the world.

This impressive store not only survives in its fiercely competitive marketplace but thrives by providing an incomparable selection of merchandise in a compelling environment—a powerful combination. Commanding the attention of residents and tourists alike, ABC Carpet & Home ranks high on New York's list of must-see retail destinations.

The May/June 2005 issue of *Furniture World* magazine profiled ABC's customer base as being affluent and loyal, with an average annual household income of $150,000. Seventy percent female, customers are well educated and culturally influential, and many own second homes. As evidence of customer loyalty, 50 percent of sales come from repeat business, making loyal customers among the store's most valuable assets. No wonder it's been successful for so many years.

BEGINNING AS A PUSHCART

In 1897, Sam and Pescha Weinrib began selling used carpet and fabrics from a pushcart on Manhattan's Lower East Side. Later, Sam's son Max opened a discount carpet store in the area. In 1961, Max's son Jerome moved the business to its current building at Broadway and East Nineteenth Street in Union Square, where it would grow into the largest rug and carpet store in the world.

For most of its existence, ABC was known throughout the Northeast as *the* place to buy broadloom carpeting for homes and businesses. That changed when Jerome's daughter Paulette Cole came aboard. In the mid-1980s, just as consumer demand for imported rugs began to escalate, Paulette and her then-partner, Evan Cole, immersed themselves in sourcing Oriental rugs. Their exposure to a diversity of artisans during their travels inspired them to acquire more than floor coverings to sell at ABC. Eventually they expanded their offerings to include an eclectic mix of bed and bath linens, antiques, furniture, lighting, gifts, and accessories. ABC Carpet & Home came to resemble a home furnishings museum exhibiting merchandise from around the world.

ABC Home pioneered the practice that is known today as cross-merchandising. Customers were encouraged to mix items from diverse parts of the world instead of purchasing complete sets of matching furniture for their homes. For many years the store has approached the business of helping people furnish their homes in a more personal way than simply selling matching living room, dining room, or bedroom suites, as do many other home furnishing retailers. The company's explanation of this concept: "ABC was a catalyst in promoting home design as a key form of self-expression, inspiring customers to create home as a personal refuge within the chaos of New York City."

ABC Carpet & Home was also among the first home furnishings stores to bring in manufacturer-owned departments. Even today the store hosts departments for Hästens, which showcases the famous Swedish maker's high-end beds; Yves Delorme, featuring luxury linens from this well-known French company; and the Silk Trading Company, offering a wide selection of quality home textiles. Designer Tom Dixon's shop, among the most recent additions, displays his innovative light fixtures and seating.

From the mid-1980s through the 1990s, the business grew and prospered, with Evan managing store operations and Paulette traveling the world to source the store's merchandise mix. Eventually, Paulette and Evan realized that their visions for the business differed. Evan wanted to expand and grow the business by opening new stores, whereas Paulette wanted to develop the Manhattan landmark into a socially responsible, mission-driven business. In 2000, Paulette chose to leave ABC to spend more time on activist and socially responsible causes. She returned to ABC in 2003 as chief executive officer and creative director of ABC Home, intent on "manifesting a retail paradigm shift where commerce is used as a vehicle and a voice." Evan went on to open H.D. Buttercup, a furniture store in Los Angeles.

Many people influence American style and fashion and in November 2007, *HFN* magazine recognized the fifty leading "Artisans of Style." Paulette Cole was number four on this list, behind Martha Stewart, Target's design team, and Gordon Segal and Barbara Turf of Crate & Barrel.

ABC Carpet & Home now occupies two buildings across the street from each other on Broadway. The 350,000 square feet of retail space features broadloom carpeting from the world's best-known mills for both home and commercial applications and an amazing array of merchandise to satisfy the tastes and interests of the most discerning home furnishings customers.

From that first pushcart, the Weinrib family built ABC Carpet & Home into one of the nation's best-known and most successful home furnishings stores. With fierce competition and a customer base that has seen it all, doing business in New York City offers real challenges. Employing a staff of over 650, ABC has established itself as *the* place for Northeastern consumers to buy home furnishings, carpeting, and imported rugs.

LET'S TAKE A TOUR

Since her return, Paulette has made some bold moves. Her ultimate goal is to make the store a 100 percent socially responsible world market offering diverse merchandise from environmentally friendly suppliers using sustainable materials. This process is likely to take several years to complete but has proven quite appealing to ABC's sophisticated customers. ABC even employs a VP of Social Responsibility, not a typical position in the retail industry. While the inventory continues to evolve to reflect this new eco-conscious mantra, many of the signs and hangtags clearly communicate what makes the merchandise different from what is sold in other stores.

The 3,500-square-foot ABC Home & Planet eco-hub on the third floor exhibits the store's sustainable products in a museum-like setting, with signage that includes descriptions of products and information on how eco-friendly, sustainable materials are used to construct specific merchandise. This area has been created to provide customers with a more thorough understanding of ecological concerns and how they relate to home furnishings. Paulette's commitment to the environment and human rights has led to the formation of the ABC Home & Planet Foundation. She uses her position and store to make a positive impact on the world.

A tour of ABC Home begins on Broadway, where passersby can

often be seen marveling at the store's elaborate window installations. The ever-changing displays often reflect mission-based themes around social and environmental justice. Layered with textiles, mirrors, embroidered pillows, ceramics, and, of course, furniture, from antiques to "good wood" (wood harvested in a sustainable manner from a healthy forest) to modern design, people enjoy a taste of what can be found inside the landmark building.

The impressive doorway of the main entrance, flanked by deities, petrified wood stumps, and dangling chandeliers, exudes a positive and powerful energy that welcomes visitors into a world apart. Chandeliers sparkle, fabrics cascade from the ceiling to look like waterfalls, and glass shelves showcase ceramics. Upon inspection of their story cards, origins range from New York–based artisans to Bolivian cooperatives. The jewelry counter is complete with recycled gold and responsibly mined diamonds from Sierra Leone. Gliding carts stacked with pillows and textiles represent global diversity, blending a romantic, feminine essence with natural earth tones in an edgy presentation. The ABC Om Apothecary offers organic and biodynamic mists, balms, and other products that help achieve balance in life.

The number of stores selling home textiles has shrunk dramatically in recent years, leaving only a few to serve the needs of home seamstresses, decorating professionals, and anyone else wanting to purchase fabrics. The Silk Trading Company's massive selection on the lower level presents hundreds of exclusive designs in every kind of fabric imaginable, including chenille, cotton, linen, mohair, silk, and velvet. This area of the store attracts not only people in the design business, including students and professional designers, but also those in entertainment who use fabrics for television shows, movies, and plays.

Upper floors house modern, contemporary, leather, and traditional wood pieces; furniture upholstered with imported fabrics; antiques; lighting; and accessories. The children's department, with its broad array of vintage and contemporary furniture for babies and young children, also offers organic baby and bath care products, out-of-the-ordinary toys from around the world, and books. The number of stores selling children's furniture has grown in recent years, but there's nothing quite like the merchandise selection and presentation at ABC Carpet & Home.

Another expansive section shows off exquisite bed and bath linens with collections of imported pillows, sheets, blankets, towels, and other bed and bath products. An area separate from the main linen department is maintained exclusively for Frette, Italy's luxury bed and bath linens company.

The visually dynamic sixth floor, which is really two stories in height and the full width of the building, features finely crafted rugs from all over the world, including India, Iran, Pakistan, Turkey, and Nepal, as well as the Madeline Weinrib Atelier. Madeline Weinrib, great-granddaughter of ABC's founder, creates contemporary textile designs used to make carpets, pillows, and various apparel products. Magnificent rugs from around the world cover the sixth-floor walls. A visit to ABC Carpet & Home is incomplete without spending some time in this department. It takes your breath away.

A TRUE DESTINATION

In addition to the everyday magic of the store, ABC creates extravagant installations, such as the monthlong "Gateway to India," which celebrated India's influence on American culture. The elaborate exhibit included saris, quilts, and window coverings made from Indian textiles. Looped documentaries were shown about India. Celebrated Indian artisans performed daily demonstrations of their crafts, master chefs from India designed a special menu, and renowned teachers led morning meditation sessions and offered Ayurvedic healing. Ayurvedic healing is holistic healing that promotes balance of body, mind, and soul. During the event, the Marigold Theater on the second floor held a speaker/presenter series featuring such visionaries as Dr. Deepak Chopra and Professor Robert Thurman, who spoke on the art, healing, and wisdom traditions of India. ABC donated 5 percent of the proceeds from "Gateway to India" sales of furniture, carpets, and deities to the William J. Clinton Foundation.

ABC customers appreciate the store not only as a unique retail experience but also as "a three-dimensional living magazine and interactive museum, including healing, education, sacntuary, theater, and art," an integral part of the company's vision.

Another part of ABC's vision is that it "aspires to present a world-mix view of organic, sustainable, beautiful, and delicious food, creating a salon for community in New York City." ABC shoppers can take a respite from all the activities to enjoy a meal in one of the several restaurant spaces within the store. Le Pain Quotidien, a European-style restaurant, prepares wonderful sandwiches, salads, soups, and pastries served to customers on long communal tables.

LONG-TERM SUCCESS

Throughout its history, ABC Carpet & Home has changed and adapted to suit the needs of its savvy customers and continues to enjoy sales increases all along the way. The store generates estimated annual sales in excess of $150 million. Most industry experts concur that ABC Carpet & Home is the largest single-location floor-covering retailer in the world. The question is, will consumers embrace and support a well-established home furnishings store in its efforts to be both socially and environmentally conscious? I wouldn't bet against Paulette Cole. Her pioneering efforts served her well in the past. I expect her passion for the environment and social issues will serve her well in the future.

ABC CARPET & HOME
888 BROADWAY
NEW YORK, NY 10003
(212) 473-3000
WWW.ABCHOME.COM

MORE PHOTOS OF ABC CARPET & HOME CAN BE SEEN AT
WWW.RETAILSUPERSTARS.COM/ABC.

In Celebration of Golf

Consumers can buy golf clubs, apparel, and other golf-related merchandise from a number of retail venues, including on-course golf shops, specialty golf stores, national sporting goods chains, and Internet merchants. With so many retail outlets all selling essentially the same merchandise, there's very little to distinguish one from another. Standing out from this sea of sameness is In Celebration of Golf, Roger Maxwell's ingenious creation in Scottsdale, Arizona.

Golf generates a passion in its players unlike any other sport. Participants in other games may be fanatical about their sport, but golfers defy logic. It's not uncommon for golfers to play in weather that might be unthinkable for other sports enthusiasts. They will travel thousands of miles to play a particular course and, if time permits, will play every day of the week.

Regardless of what age one takes up the game, golfers can play well into their later years. It's not uncommon for golfers to play into their eighties and even nineties. Skills may wane but passion for the game, owning the best equipment, and playing different courses never do. When compared to lovers of other sports, the most avid golfers frequently spend a disproportionate amount of money on equipment and traveling to play their favorite courses around the world.

This should be good news for those in the business. Unfortunately, as in other retail segments of late, the number of stores selling golf merchandise has decreased significantly, leaving the bulk of the business under the control of a few large sporting goods and specialty golf retail chains. According to research recently conducted by *Golf Digest* magazine, the total number of off-course golf retail stores has shrunk by 25 percent over the last five years. During this same period of time, the overall square footage devoted to golf retail increased by 7 percent, attributable to large chains opening more stores.

A scenario such as this provides a great opportunity for a truly distinctive golf retailer to capture the dollars and loyalty of golfers. That's exactly what Roger Maxwell has done with In Celebration of Golf. His concept is to provide a shopping experience built around the traditions and history of the game, sell only the highest-quality products, and provide a level of customer service that caters to the passions evoked by the game.

A UNIQUE RETAIL ENVIRONMENT

In Celebration of Golf, at 13,000 square feet, looks and feels much like the clubhouse of an old, well-established country club one might find in the Northeast. "Caddies" clad in the same white coverall-type uniforms worn by those at the Masters Tournament greet customers as they enter the store and provide a scorecard that serves as a map to the various departments.

Most stores rely on merchandise differentiation and a few signs to distinguish one department from another. In Celebration of Golf separates its departments, or "Celebrations," based on golf-related themes employing distinctive carpeting, wall coverings, lighting, and fixtures to support the theme. Not only does this make each Celebration easily identifiable, it also shows off the merchandise in an inviting environment and piques customer interest.

LET'S TAKE A TOUR

Customers enter the store into an open area called The First Tee. This front part of the store also serves as the checkout where customers complete their purchases at a circular-shaped counter. The Players Room, located to the right of The First Tee, displays signature clothing lines named for some of the game's most prominent players. The selection includes designs from the Bobby Jones, Tiger Woods, Ben Hogan, Jack Nicklaus, and Greg Norman lines of golf apparel. Just off to the side of The Players Room customers enter The Trophy Presentation where they can have their purchases gift wrapped in golf-themed papers and bows. Roger describes this as a "Celebration in which your purchases become your trophies."

In The Men's and Women's Professional's Shops, just beyond The Players Room, one can select from a diverse array of quality men's and women's golf and casual clothing and accessories. Customers who belong to exclusive country clubs or frequent upscale resorts may have been exposed to well-merchandised apparel displays, but it's unlikely they will have experienced such a wide range of designer brands so beautifully presented as is done at In Celebration of Golf. A merchandising imperative when presenting high-quality products to discerning consumers is to make the merchandise the star. In Celebration of Golf takes great care to show every item to its best advantage so it is attractive and inviting to the customer.

Tucked into the left side of The Men's and Women's Professional's Shops sits The Antiquities of the Game Celebration, built to have the look of a quaint European antique shop filled with items representing the history of golf. Merchandise seen here includes old-time wood-shafted golf clubs, trophies from bygone tournaments, rare books, assorted golf memorabilia, and a collection of autographed golf balls. Customers consider this Celebration one of the store's special treasures.

Next comes The Spike Shop, housing a huge selection of quality golf footwear. At last count shoppers could choose from more than 1,000 pairs of men's and women's golf shoes in every kind of material, color, and style. Both The Professional's Shop and The Spike Shop display merchandise in elegant wood cabinetry and fixtures. The Spike Shop fixtures look like the large, wooden members' lockers found in classic country clubs around the United States.

Cushy golf-themed sofas and chairs in this area front a large-screen, high-definition television always tuned to either the Golf Channel or the latest tournament coverage. On a table in the center lie several issues of the most recent golf publications from around the world. Also available for customers' enjoyment are fresh-brewed coffee, soft drinks, and cookies for snacking. Roger thinks of this as "The Have-Way House."

Retailers continually search for ways to keep customers in their stores longer, the strategy being: the longer customers stay in a store, the more they will buy. While customers already spend a great deal of time in this store because there is so much to see, the availability of a big-screen television, magazines, beverages, and snacks encourages customers to get comfortable and stay as long as they want.

The Practice Tee and Club Room can be found in the rear left corner of the Celebration. Using a golf simulator, customers can try out clubs from the top manufacturers in the golf business. Next is The Golfer's Den, which features golf-themed home furnishings, such as large comfortable chairs, tables, cabinetry, lamps, and accessories to embellish the golfer's home.

The impeccably clean men's and women's locker rooms, located near the middle of the left side, replicate those at the Augusta National Golf Club, where the Masters Tournament takes place each spring. "We include a tribute to the past winners of the Masters," Roger explains, "by hanging a green jacket for each winner since 1995, the year In Celebration of Golf opened for business." Continuing down the hallway past the restrooms, customers enjoy The Cobbler's Workbench, designed to look like an old-fashioned golf-club maker's workshop. Seated at the workbench, a Disneyland-like Animatronic clubmaker describes the craft of assembling golf clubs as it was practiced in the early years of the last century.

With retail space being so valuable today, rarely does a merchant willingly use it for anything other than displaying something to sell. A most unusual aspect of In Celebration of Golf is that it devotes a great deal of space to nonselling functions that enhance ambiance and the customer's experience. The Cobbler's Workbench counts as one such feature, there to provide a bit of history, entertainment, and romance.

The next Celebration is The Art of the Game, named appropriately for the artwork displayed. Rivaling a fine art gallery, this area exhibits over 400 framed pieces of golf art and memorabilia, including original oil paintings, watercolors, lithographs, serigraphs, sculptures, photographs, and posters. A number of one-of-a-kind pieces displayed here represent golf's most celebrated artists. Also available for purchase are autographed photos and flags from golf tournaments signed by the player who won. Everything reflects the game and the enthusiast's love of all things golf. Customers are unlikely to find a better selection of golf-related art to enhance their home or office.

To the left of The Art of the Game customers come upon Ye Old Golf Shoppe, probably the largest and most comprehensive collection of golf-related giftware, accessories, and books gathered in one place anywhere. The treasures in this Celebration range from barware, chess sets, and greeting cards to handbags, golf games, and picture frames—a trove of over 700 truly unique golf-themed items from around the world.

Kathy Maxwell, Roger's wife, searches out the merchandise and provides the inspiration behind Ye Old Golf Shoppe. Her passion for selecting just the right products is reflected in the faces of awestruck first-time visitors. Shoppers find it nearly impossible to visit this store and not take home several items from Ye Old Golf Shoppe.

I've never known a retailer more committed to staying true to his concept and business principles than Roger Maxwell. In Celebration of Golf is today exactly what he envisioned it would be back in the early 1990s, with only minor changes to keep up with customer expectations and needs.

REDEFINING A TIRED RETAIL SEGMENT

Roger spent years as a PGA professional before becoming vice president of Marriott's worldwide golf operations. In his years with Marriott, he pioneered many of the merchandising concepts now integral to the golf industry. He earned a reputation in the golf and hospitality industries not only as a merchandising expert, but also as a premier provider of outstanding customer experiences at Marriott's highly respected golf resort properties.

The golf industry has never had the reputation of being on the cutting edge when it comes to retail operations. Many golf merchants let decades pass without changing fixtures and display furniture. With a few exceptions, it is common to see merchandising methods used in golf shops and stores that have long been abandoned by other retail segments.

Roger incorporates his unsurpassed merchandising abilities and penchant for customer service into the core culture of In Celebration of Golf. Owing to his unrivaled eye for detail, customers will never see a burned-out lightbulb, dust on a fixture, apparel in disarray, or cluttered displays. He and his staff exemplify this commitment to detail with everything they do, from merchandise presentation and customer service to follow-up and store cleanliness. All of this contributes to In Celebration of Golf's singular success.

EXECUTING A STRATEGY

It's not enough in today's fiercely competitive environment to depend solely on unique, high-quality merchandise to distinguish a store from the competition. Customer focus glues the strategy together at In Celebration of Golf. From the caddy/greeter and knowledgeable, courteous sales associates to beautifully appointed restrooms and an efficient checkout, every part of the customer experience is pleasantly memorable.

Even with all the glitz and glamour that customers experience in life these days, In Celebration of Golf still astonishes, amazes, and delights them when they walk through the door. Creating a highly focused and visually dynamic store requires a comprehensive viewpoint of the business of retailing. At In Celebration of Golf the visual elements take a floor-to-ceiling approach to the layout and design, lighting that enhances the merchandise rather than simply illuminating the entire store, and features such as The Cobbler's Workbench, a display that doesn't actually sell anything but adds to the overall shopping experience for the customer. The combination of a visually dynamic store focused on a targeted group of consumers with a great selection of merchandise and unrivaled customer service makes an unbeatable strategy.

In addition to the Scottsdale store, the Celebration staff manages golf operations and shops at several golf courses in and around the Phoenix area. There are also a growing number of small In Celebration of Golf stores located in airports across the country. These satellite stores offer an edited selection of the same quality golf apparel, accessories, and gifts found in the original store.

Roger and his staff excel at keeping In Celebration of Golf looking fresh and interesting for customers every day of the year. While Scottsdale attracts more visitors during the winter months, customers can visit this shop any time of the year and find pristine conditions and the merchandise artfully displayed. Due to economic pressures in the off-season, it has become common for retailers to pare inventory to such a degree that customers no longer have the choices they would have during "high season." That will never be the situation at In Celebration of Golf. Customers always have a complete experience in every Celebration of the store, even in the hottest summer months when tourists and residents are less likely to be in Arizona.

When it comes to the task of retail execution, In Celebration of Golf ranks among the best stores of any kind anywhere in America. It also happens to be a fun place to visit, whether you are a golfer or not.

In Celebration of Golf

7001 N. Scottsdale Road, Suite 172

Scottsdale, Arizona 85253

(480) 951-4444

www.celebrategolf.com

More photos of In Celebration of Golf can be seen at
www.retailsuperstars.com/celebrategolf.

Gallery Furniture

For many reasons furniture has been one segment of retailing not dominated by giant national chains. While several chains have tried, the costs associated with opening, stocking, and operating enough stores to dominate the category have been prohibitive. It's a tough, competitive business. In just the last few years we have seen a number of home furnishings retailers fail, including Wickes, Jennifer Convertibles, and Mattress Discounters. Even with these failures, no lack of furniture stores exists in America, but most are independents or local and regional chains. While many small and midsize furniture retailers do an adequate job serving their communities, there's little to distinguish one from another. Not so with Gallery Furniture. Gallery is unique.

How can a big-city furniture store selling primarily moderately priced merchandise be considered one of a kind? The only characteristic Gallery Furniture shares with its competitors is that it generally sells moderately priced furniture. In fact, Gallery Furniture doesn't just sell furniture. Owner Jim (better known as Mack) McIngvale does just about everything differently from other furniture retailers. This contrary approach to furniture retailing results in an estimated $150 million in sales annually.

A LITTLE BACKGROUND

I first met Mack several years ago at a Texas Retailers Association meeting where we were both speakers. I looked forward to meeting the retailer known around Houston as "Mattress Mack." We had a nice chat, and a few weeks later he invited me to come to Houston to see his store.

All I'd heard about Gallery Furniture at that point was that the store and its owner were wildly successful. I didn't know the store consisted of a collection of funky old buildings strung together with tents and crammed with furniture. I didn't know the store at that time generated $75 million in annual sales—an extraordinary amount for a single store in the furniture business. Mack and his store were outselling every furniture store in Texas and beyond, and I was eager to find out why.

FROM HUMBLE BEGINNINGS

Mack and his wife, Linda, arrived in Houston in 1981 with $5,000 and their dream to open a furniture store. First they needed a

building, but all they could find that was affordable was a dilapi-
dated and long-abandoned model home on Southwest Freeway.
Although this less-than-grand building was not exactly what they
envisioned their first store to be, they were determined to make it
work. The McIngvales used their meager funds and some merchandise provided on consignment to stock their "store." That first year
they sold $1 million worth of furniture, $2 million the second—they
were on their way.

It wasn't long before they needed more space than the original
model home could provide, so they took over the two other model
homes on the property. When they ran out of room again, they strung
semipermanent tents among the three buildings. This allowed them
to display a lot more merchandise. The first time I saw this sprawling
maze of tents and buildings, I thought it looked more like a Bedouin
village in the Sahara than one of America's most successful furniture
stores. Yet, out of this unusual conglomeration of buildings and tents,
the McIngvales built a furniture business unrivaled in the United
States. After years in those old model homes and tents, Gallery
Furniture moved into a 100,000-square-foot store built across the
parking lot. After the move into the new store the old buildings
came down, providing a larger, much needed parking lot.

The growth and success of Gallery Furniture can be attributed to
Mack's dedication, incredible energy, entrepreneurial spirit, vision,
and a willingness to change the way furniture retailing had been
done. Among the most admirable attributes of this amazing retailer
is his desire and ability to embrace new methods of doing business
and finding merchandise and services that will delight his customers.
With his uncompromising commitment to hard work, it's easy to see
why Gallery has been successful through tough economic times, se-
vere weather, and Houston's fiercely competitive marketplace.

Certainly other successful single-location furniture stores exist,
but none have achieved success in quite the same way or to the degree
as Gallery Furniture. For years, while operating out of its unusual
conglomeration of buildings and tents, Gallery generated more sales
than any other independent furniture store in the United States.

MATTRESS MACK

When Houston's oil boom went bust in 1983, many local retail companies failed, unemployment ran rampant, and sales at Gallery Furniture plummeted. Mack had to do something, so he invested all his marketing dollars in TV advertising.

Knowing he needed something outrageous to grab the attention of viewers, he removed the insides of a twin-size mattress, cut holes for his head, arms, and feet, and wore the mattress like a suit while filming his commercials. Low-budget and definitely a little tacky, Mack stood in front of the camera wearing that mattress, and he talked about Gallery's great furniture. He ended every commercial with what's become his signature line: "Gallery Furniture Saves You Money!" More than once the marketing students at the University of Houston voted Gallery Furniture commercials the worst TV ads in Houston. Yet Mack's decidedly unsophisticated and enthusiastic approach to advertising attracts thousands of customers into the store every year, and they buy hundreds of millions of dollars in furniture. To this day, he is affectionately known to many Texans as "Mattress Mack."

OUTRAGEOUS PROMOTIONS

Mack is a tireless promoter and one of the best marketers I know. One year, he decided he wanted a Christmas tree larger than the one in New York's Rockefeller Center. After an exhaustive search, he found a 105-foot Norwegian spruce for which he paid $120,000. He had the tree shipped to Houston from Saratoga Springs, New York. Decorated with 30,000 lightbulbs, tons of tinsel, and topped with a giant gold star, he boasted the world's largest Christmas tree. Visitors came from all over South Texas to see that tree, and, oh yes, shop for furniture.

Mack ties many of his promotional events to his interest in sports and the popularity of Houston's sports teams. He was the first local, independent retailer to sponsor a nationally televised college bowl game. The game between Texas Tech and East Carolina universities in late 2000, titled Gallery Furniture.com Bowl, put Gallery's marketing message in front of consumers from coast to coast.

Mack and Gallery Furniture became well known because of the massive number of television and radio commercials run on local stations every day. As Houston's population has grown and become more diverse, Mack wisely runs commercials on Hispanic radio and television stations, establishing Gallery as the primary destination for Spanish-speaking furniture and consumer electronics shoppers in South Texas. By one estimate, Gallery Furniture spends as much as $10 million on advertising annually.

SERVING ALL CONSUMERS

For much of its existence, Gallery focused its merchandise selection on consumers who required moderately priced furniture and time payments. But the store also attracted a small but loyal group of affluent customers. A few years ago Mack broadened his merchandise selection to better serve the needs of this more affluent population. He started by adding the Tempur-Pedic line of mattresses, the average price of which is nearly $3,000. These beds became an instant hit, earning Gallery Furniture recognition as Tempur-Pedic's highest volume single-store retailer.

On the heels of Gallery's success selling higher-end beds followed two other merchandise brand additions meant to attract discerning, more affluent consumers. The first was the installation of a Hästens bedding gallery featuring the complete line from this famous Swedish bed manufacturer. The Hästens gallery provides a level of sophistication in the store not previously attained. Hästens beds, priced from $4,300 to more than $50,000, appeal to customers Gallery had only occasionally seen in the past.

The second step was to become the exclusive Kreiss home furnishings retailer in the Houston area. Kreiss makes a broad range of luxury contemporary furniture, accessories, and linens. Fewer than twenty Kreiss dealers exist in the United States, so owning dealership rights for Houston would give Gallery exclusivity of the brand. Mack bought out the existing Kreiss dealer operating out of a store in the Galleria Shopping Center and built a complete Kreiss department in Gallery Furniture. Affluent consumers can now buy high-end furniture and benefit from Gallery Furniture's same-day delivery promise. The ability to deliver merchandise the same day is extremely rare in high-end furniture stores.

By adding the upscale lines of Tempur-Pedic, Hästens, and Kreiss to the store's existing selection of moderately priced furniture, Gallery has now positioned itself to serve the diverse needs of every furniture buyer in the Houston marketplace.

ALWAYS A SURPRISE

Gallery Furniture may have become one of the country's largest independent retailers working out of those funky old buildings and tents, but the 100,000-square-foot store that houses Gallery today is way more than a big furniture store. Over the years Mack acquired sports, entertainment, and celebrity memorabilia that's proven to be a hit with customers. He's built dozens of attractions in the store featuring his collections, and they delight customers both young and old. The "shoppertainment" elements of this store make it a popular destination for the whole family. While children might find shopping in a furniture store somewhat boring, that is not the case at Gallery. There are lots of features to keep them interested and entertained.

Sports memorabilia displayed in glass cases throughout the store includes footballs and basketballs from championship games, and jerseys worn by some of the best-known NBA players of recent years. A display of Shaquille O'Neal's massive size 22 basketball shoes certainly attracts attention. But there's so much more, and it's not just sports stuff.

Shoppers can see Elvis Presley's famous white Lincoln Continental convertible, a NASCAR race car, plus several other exotic sports cars. There's a giant Trojan horse towering over the children's department, a water-driven paddle wheel, and a cage filled with talking parrots. The Princess Diana exhibit ranks among the most popular. Mack built a small castle within the store to house Diana's famous jewels among other Diana-related memorabilia, as well as information about her life.

Customers love going to Gallery Furniture because the visual features and shopping experience enhancements constantly change. Past attractions included a bowling alley, a tennis court, a jungle theme in the children's furniture section, and a giant 450-inch television screen. Recent additions incorporate sports-themed home theater rooms fully outfitted with the latest audio and video equipment. A visit to Gallery Furniture always surprises customers.

WAIT UNTIL YOU SEE THE RESTROOMS

Several years ago Mack read a book about one-of-a-kind restrooms from around the world and decided Gallery should have its own one-of-a-kind restrooms. He converted the traditional men's and women's multistall restrooms in the front showroom area into small, individual, themed restrooms, each one unique. The themes include sports—basketball, golf, and tennis—as well as old-time movies. A video screen mounted in every restroom plays movies or sporting events, and the decor incorporates posters, photos, wallpaper, and accessories to support the theme.

AND THERE'S FOOD AND FREE STUFF

Restaurants and fast-food venues may be fairly common in stores these days, but Gallery takes it to a new level. A professional chef and his staff provide hundreds of home-cooked meals every day—all at no cost to the customers or employees. That's right, free!

Giveaway items fill several baskets behind the front counter. Virtually any purchase at Gallery Furniture qualifies for a free gift. It could be a T-shirt, basketball, sports bag, or oversize tennis balls, all with the Gallery Furniture logo prominently displayed. Every year Gallery gives away hundreds of thousands of these items. It is not uncommon to see kids on a Houston playground wearing Gallery Furniture T-shirts playing with a Gallery Furniture ball. These give-away items are part of the appeal and just one of the reasons so many families with children regularly visit the store.

GALLERY FURNITURE BREAKS ALL TRADITIONS

Typically customers go into a furniture store, pick out what they want, order it, and then wait as long as twelve weeks to get it. Why does it take so long? It's costly to warehouse vast amounts of furniture, so many furniture retailers don't order from the manufacturer until a sale is made. Often the furniture isn't even constructed until the manufacturer receives the order from the retailer. In an instant-gratification society, this tradition does not fare well with customers. Even if a retailer stocks the furniture, delivery may not happen for several more days—until the schedule puts the truck in a particular area of town. No sense of urgency exists for retailers in the furniture business.

That's not the way it's done at Gallery. Every Gallery Furniture delivery is made by Gallery Furniture personnel in Gallery Furniture trucks. But the thing that distinguishes Gallery's furniture-buying experience from that of every other furniture store in America is this: IF YOU BUY IT TODAY, YOU GET IT TODAY! Gallery can do this because it maintains a complete stock of everything displayed on the showroom floor in its warehouse, which is located directly behind the store.

Since most customers want their furniture right away, the policy of same-day delivery gives Gallery a distinct competitive edge. A simple yet powerful slogan has come from this. On giant billboards all over town, Houstonians see the word TODAY printed above the Gallery Furniture logo. The TODAY slogan can be found on everything from print advertising to the shirts Gallery employees wear to work.

Mack's TODAY policy has long been a thorn in the side of competing furniture retailers. Others have tried it but can't quite get it right. One retailer recently advertised "Instant Delivery," but ended up scheduling several days out. Not quite instant.

Traditionally the retail furniture business employs commissioned salespeople and offers other financial incentives. If a particular brand or item affords the retailer a higher profit margin, salespeople who sell that product receive a financial incentive, commonly known as a spiff. So that's what the salesperson will attempt to sell first, over nonspiffed merchandise. The push to sell the spiffed item may be so strong that customers don't always get what best meets their furniture wants and needs. Gallery's salespeople receive straight salaries and are expected to take the time to ensure every customer gets exactly the right furniture to meet their specific wants and needs.

Noncommissioned salespeople and same-day deliveries are just two of the ways Gallery Furniture stands out in a sea of ordinary furniture stores bound by tradition.

EXCEEDING RETAIL METRICS

Retailing utilizes plenty of tools for measuring and evaluating success. For retailers who sell higher-ticket products such as furniture, the two most widely used metrics are dollars per square foot and inventory turns. Each year *Furniture Today,* the leading industry publication, recognizes the top 100 furniture stores in America based on total sales volume. Gallery Furniture usually ranks near the middle of this group of mostly multiple-store companies. But no one even comes close to Gallery's store performance.

Among the elite group of top 100 furniture retailers, the average sales per square foot generally falls just under $300. Gallery Furniture consistently tops that at $1,600 per square foot. The average number of inventory turns each year for the top 100 group falls between four and five. Gallery Furniture moves inventory at an astounding rate— 22 to 23 turns per year. The numbers reflect one simple truth: Gallery Furniture outperforms every other furniture store in America.

CHARITY AND PROMOTIONS

Wearing a mattress certainly got the attention of furniture buyers in Houston, but Mack's fame has spread further due to his involvement in many of the most prominent charitable events in his community and throughout Texas.

Several times Mack purchased the prizewinning steer at the annual Houston Livestock Show, with proceeds going to the Livestock Show College Scholarship Fund. He generously provides funds and equipment to colleges and police departments and donates new furniture to teachers for their school lounges.

He doesn't hesitate to provide new furniture to people affected by natural disasters, including families who suffered after hurricanes Katrina and Rita in 2005 and Ike in 2008. Following the tsunami in Southeast Asia, the McIngvales partnered with former presidents George H. W. Bush and Bill Clinton and successfully collected relief funds for those impacted by the disaster.

Gallery's Annual Christmas Giveaway may be one of the most generous things I've ever seen from a retailer. Pre-holiday TV commercials invite Houstonians to nominate people to win a houseful of new furniture. A committee of community leaders determines, from over 8,000 letters received each year, those who are most deserving. They select fifteen families to be helped by Mack and Gallery Furniture. Often it is a complete surprise to the winners when the Gallery delivery truck pulls up to their home. This annual event has been helping families in need for over two decades.

Mack has made several significant donations to Texas Children's Hospital. Recently he contributed $400,000 to the hospital's Center for Childhood Obesity, the Adolescent Medicine Clinic, and the Sports Medicine Clinic. He also signed on to help in the hospital's fight to solve the child obesity problem.

INSPIRATION TO YOUNG AND OLD

Mack's generosity encompasses more than just financial aid. Several days a week he makes speeches at no charge to clubs, schools, churches, and other such organizations about what it takes to be successful in life. He's a highly accomplished speaker with a passion for his message. People young and old relate to him.

One evening he was leaving a restaurant in Houston when a young man in his late twenties approached, introduced himself, and shook Mack's hand. He said, "You don't know me, Mr. McIngvale, but back when I was a teenager you spoke at my school. At the time I was doing drugs, getting in trouble, and generally not doing much of anything worthwhile. Your speech so inspired me that I knuckled down in school and graduated. Today I'm married and have a good job. Your speech was the inspiration. Thank you."

Someone once asked why he does all these things. He does them because he genuinely cares about giving back to the community— the community in which he lived his dreams; the community that helped Gallery Furniture become the most successful single-store furniture retailer in America.

Mack and Gallery Furniture have enjoyed tremendous success by breaking tradition with everyone else in the furniture business. Rather than looking solely within the furniture industry to set his standards, Mack has always looked at the entire retail industry, asking, "What do the best retailers do that we don't do?" This approach gives him a broader sense of what he must do to improve his business and stand out. You can be sure he will continue to follow his instincts and boldly move his business forward.

GALLERY FURNITURE

6006 N. FREEWAY

HOUSTON, TX 77076

(713) 694-5570

WWW.GALLERYFURNITURE.COM

MORE PHOTOS OF GALLERY FURNITURE CAN BE SEEN AT
WWW.RETAILSUPERSTARS.COM/GALLERY.

Wilkes Bashford

San Francisco,
California

Every big city in America supports stores serving the
needs of affluent consumers whose tastes and interests
demand high-quality designer apparel. Few merchants are
as connected to or have more influence on a city's well-
heeled, fashion-conscious consumer than San Francisco's
Wilkes Bashford. Wilkes Bashford, the store, directly reflects its namesake owner. Both exude taste, elegance, re-
finement, and sophistication, and both significantly impact
the business of fashion.

THE BEGINNING

San Francisco, circa 1966, was a destination for young adults whose alternative lifestyles were decidedly casual and whose mantra was "Sex, drugs, and rock and roll." This wild, not necessarily proud time in this nation's history saw Levi's jeans and T-shirts supplant designer fashions for most young people. At the same time, a number of department stores, long established in San Francisco, sold traditional men's and women's apparel from old-line clothing brands but offered little in the way of better-quality, fashionable merchandise. Instead they catered to the middle of the marketplace, sticking to apparel that appealed to middle-class consumers.

In August of 1966, Wilkes Bashford, who had garnered his experience from working at Federated Department Stores in Ohio and the White House department store in San Francisco, opened his own shop. What distinguished it from the very beginning was Wilkes's refined taste and ability to select stylish, fashion-forward apparel of the highest quality. "Fashion forward" wasn't part of the lexicon in those days, yet this exceptional merchant connected with fashion-conscious San Franciscans and sold merchandise not available elsewhere in the Bay Area. From the very beginning he worked at ensuring that the selection included a mix of high-end designers, top-brand names, and exclusive private-label merchandise.

The original store measured 2,400 square feet and sold men's apparel exclusively. Then in 1978, Wilkes added women's apparel. By the early 1980s the store had grown to 18,500 square feet and was located on the ground floor of a multistory parking lot building owned by the City of San Francisco. A bitter rent dispute with the city ensued, culminating in his moving the store to a building across the street, where Wilkes Bashford thrives to this day.

ON THE CUTTING EDGE OF FASHION

Wilkes possesses an uncanny talent for spotting apparel trends and the potential of new designers before they've made their mark on the fashion world. His was the first store in the United States to sell Italian designer Ermenegildo Zegna's fashions that today clothe the most discerning businessmen, politicians, athletes, and celebrities. In 1968 Wilkes bought a selection of wide ties from an unknown designer in New York's Empire State Building. The ties sold quickly in the store for the then unheard-of price of $12.50. This was the West Coast's first exposure to Ralph Lauren's creations.

Wilkes has built and maintained his place on the cutting edge of the fashion business, offering menswear from such designers as Giorgio Armani, Gianfranco Ferré, and Gianni Versace well before other stores recognized the opportunity. Meticulously tailored Brioni suits imported from Italy have been a part of the store's inventory from the beginning. In the 1960s a Brioni suit sold for around $350. Today an off-the-rack Brioni sells for approximately $5,000. Custom-tailored Brioni suits command substantially more. His good taste and understanding of what wealthy customers will buy have been proven year after year for the last four decades.

In large companies, inspiration, guidance, and leadership come from many people. In small retail businesses, inspiration, guidance, and leadership nearly always come from the owner. Now in his seventies, Wilkes Bashford continues to inspire, guide, and lead those who work for him. Among the most daunting challenges fashion retailers face is balancing inventory to meet the needs of a wide range of customers—from young to old, fashion-forward to classically conservative. Wilkes and his staff proficiently maintain that balance. His long hours, six-day weeks, and involvement in the everyday details of operating the business attest to his ongoing commitment to retail excellence—the cornerstone of his success.

ELEGANT AND STYLISH

The Wilkes Bashford store occupies a seven-story, 28,500-square-foot building just off San Francisco's famous Union Square. In addition to providing the finest men's and women's apparel, the store's lower level, dubbed Wilkes Home, affords customers a selective assortment of decorator items, antiques, accessories, and imported bed linens.

The main floor displays men's trousers, sport coats, shoes, and the Kiton gallery. Exquisitely cut suits and other items from this famous Italian menswear maker hold a premium merchandising position on the entrance level. Women relish the selection of couture, luxury sportswear, handbags, and shoes on the second floor. The store's Brioni shop, along with men's suit lines and formalwear, take up the third floor. The fourth floor is devoted to men's furnishings and classic sportswear, and women's sportswear is on the fifth floor.

Well-to-do consumers come to expect above-the-norm amenities and services, and Wilkes Bashford complies to the fullest. Wet bars situated on each floor provide a full complement of drinks, along with fresh coffee throughout the day. Business and administrative offices share the top floor with a charming salon reserved for those patrons who prefer to make apparel selections in private. Refreshments catered by San Francisco's chic Campton Place Hotel add to the level of service this discerning customer expects from a store selling luxury apparel. Complimentary gift wrapping artistically applied and home delivery complete the experience.

The men's dressing rooms at Wilkes Bashford are large and comfortable, with floor-to-ceiling mirrors. The women's dressing rooms, also spacious and comfortable, provide mirrors on all sides. Mirrors liberally placed throughout the departments allow customers the convenience of seeing how something looks wherever they happen to be in the store. Among the most significant improvements in retailing—and more specifically luxury retailing—in recent years is lighting. Wilkes Bashford appropriately places subdued lighting in dressing rooms and throughout the store so that patrons of all ages look their very best.

Instead of large open spaces commonly found in stores offering such a wide selection of merchandise, Wilkes Bashford uses walls, fixtures, and tasteful merchandise displays to break up the rooms on each floor. The classy and understated decor perfectly showcases the fashionable merchandise. This tactic ensures a more intimate shopping environment, and customers don't feel at all overpowered by the size of the store. Wilkes Bashford is simply one of the most stunning and exquisitely displayed stores you will see anywhere.

A WELL-KNOWN RETAILER
AND HIS TWO FAMOUS FRIENDS

Some friendships can prove most fortuitous when it comes to publicity for a merchant. Wilkes Bashford, the store, has enjoyed considerable success because of its owner's unwavering commitment to excellence, but his friendship with two of San Francisco's most famous citizens hasn't hurt.

Early on in his political and law career, former California state assemblyman Willie Brown discovered the store, its stylish apparel, and charismatic owner. Willie and Wilkes came to be friends. As Willie's fame spread and good taste in clothes was publicized, so, too, did awareness of Wilkes Bashford's store. By the time San Francisco elected Willie Brown mayor, his penchant for meticulously tailored suits was widely known, as was the source of said suits—his friend's store.

Wilkes counted the world-famous *San Francisco Chronicle* columnist Herb Caen—another connoisseur of fine clothing—as a close friend as well. For many years Caen's must-read daily column revealed celebrity sightings, offered opinions, spread gossip, and issued commentary concerning the goings-on in this cosmopolitan city. Beginning in 1974, Wilkes Bashford, Willie Brown, and Herb Caen, along with three other friends, lunched together every Friday at Le

Central, San Francisco's famed bistro. The topics debated at these lively luncheons often turned up in Caen's daily column, as well as the names of those in attendance, including Wilkes Bashford, owner of the incomparable clothing store so named. In an article in *Town & Country* magazine, then-mayor Willie Brown had this to say about Wilkes Bashford's store: "You don't go there out of desperation, you go for inspiration."

Wilkes Bashford has had his share of famous customers frequent the store, including former secretary of state George Shultz, record executive Clive Davis, and movie star/California governor Arnold Schwarzenegger.

RECOGNITION FROM THE FASHION COMMUNITY

On numerous occasions Wilkes Bashford has been recognized for his contributions to the industry by such apparel publications as *Menswear Retailer (MR)*, *Daily News Record (DNR)*, and *Women's Wear Daily*. *Esquire* and *Harper's Bazaar* magazines consistently include the store among "100 of America's Leading Retailers" and "The Best Specialty Stores in America," respectively. *DNR* has also included Wilkes Bashford on its list of the "50 Most Influential Menswear Stores." Stores qualifying for these honors must continually be style leaders providing exceptional customer service to discerning customers. On every level Wilkes Bashford exemplifies these qualifications.

MEDIOCRITY VS. EXCELLENCE

As retailing evolves into more of a commodity business and the economy struggles, merchants are forced to do everything they can to cut operating costs, reduce the number of associates needed to operate the business, stock merchandise that fits the most popular price points, and, finally, acquiesce to mediocrity in service. Fortunately, in this commoditized retail world, merchants exist who refuse to give in to this way of thinking. They remain dedicated to high-quality merchandise, exceptional service, and great attention to detail as a means to growth and sustenance. Wilkes Bashford offers a clear alternative to commodity retailing.

With over forty years of success, Wilkes Bashford serves the fashionable elite from all around Northern California. Affluent consumers expect more than good service—they expect great service. They appreciate retailers who understand and care about their individual wants, needs, and expectations.

Unlike stores in which salespeople work in a specific department, Wilkes Bashford's sales staff performs more like personal shoppers showing customers merchandise throughout the store. With an average tenure of nineteen years, the Wilkes Bashford sales staff is exceptionally knowledgeable and understanding of customer preferences. The staff ranks among the store's most valuable assets.

Anyone who appreciates beautiful clothes and exquisite stores will love Wilkes Bashford. This store unquestionably sets the standard and enjoys being at the pinnacle of retailing. Unlike many retailers, Wilkes Bashford does not look to cash in on the latest fads, but rather provides the store's well-heeled customers with just the right merchandise for their fashion needs. It may be a different way of doing business, but it has proven sustainable for many years.

WILKES BASHFORD
375 SUTTER STREET
SAN FRANCISCO, CA 94108
(415) 986-4380
WWW.WILKESBASHFORD.COM

MORE PHOTOS OF WILKES BASHFORD CAN BE SEEN AT
WWW.RETAILSUPERSTARS.COM/WILKESBASHFORD.

Nell Hill's

The Midwestern town of Atchison, Kansas, is home to Nell Hill's, a store one would not expect to find in such a small rural community with a population of just 10,000. Yet this remarkable retailer sells millions of dollars' worth of quality home furnishings annually. Atchison once claimed fame as the birthplace of aviator Amelia Earhart, but today it is far better known for the exceptional Nell Hill's home furnishings store.

The attraction to Nell Hill's has nothing to do with location. Customers travel from miles around in their quest for out-of-the-ordinary home furnishings, china, cookware, and decorative accessories. A good number drive from Kansas City, more than an hour away, but it's not uncommon to find customers from all across the United States browsing the store's wares.

What compels customers to make such a trek? The merchandise at Nell Hill's captivates shoppers to such a degree that when they find something they want, they literally MUST have it. Shoppers sort through displays filled with distinctive "must-have" home furnishings unavailable elsewhere at prices to suit every budget. Choices range from a few dollars for unique Christmas ornaments to several thousand for highly desirable European antiques. The inspiration behind this extraordinary store is proprietor Mary Carol Garrity. With unsurpassed taste, creativity, and style, Mary Carol seeks out home decor items that are different from those usually found in stores of this kind.

At Nell Hill's, delighting the customer takes precedence over everything else. Unlike large retail chains that select inventory to fill price points or assure high profit-margins, Mary Carol bases merchandise selection in her store solely on customer appeal. She knows her customers and what items they surely will fall in love with. She brings to mind the Energizer Bunny, constantly on the go. Not only does she determine what to sell in the store, she also creates merchandise displays, helps customers with decorating ideas, and writes books on decorating and entertaining. In recent years she and her store have become one of the country's most important influences shaping lifestyle, home decor, and entertainment choices and tastes.

RETAILING IS IN HER BLOOD

Mary Carol grew up in a retailing family. Her parents operated a clothing store for thirty-five years, and she began helping out when she was eleven years old. At this tender age, she fell in love with the retail business, looking forward to seeing the sales numbers at the end of each day. It was in her blood.

In partnership with her father, Mary Carol established Nell Hill's in 1981. The small store initially sold cheeses, teas, and biscuits, as well as kitchen accessories. From this modest beginning, she added other merchandise categories and expanded the store to accommodate the additional merchandise. Eventually she eliminated gourmet foods altogether. Today, this unimposing store is crammed with an amazing array of home decor and kitchen merchandise that nearly defies description.

AN EXPANDING RETAIL ENTERPRISE

Attesting to her success, Mary Carol's retail business comprises more than a single store, and it continues to grow. Nell Hill's, the original, was named for her maternal grandmother and occupies a 9,000-square-foot, two-story building.

Just a few doors down on Commercial Street resides G. Diebolts, named after her father. This 2,500-square-foot former bank building with thirty-foot ceilings and classic architecture now showcases a wide selection of bed linens and home textiles. Artistically staged beds exhibit a variety of designs from basic to elegant. Customers can see exactly how these goods will look in their homes.

Around the corner from Nell Hill's on Fifth Street, shoppers find Garrity's Encore in Atchison's former Masonic temple, built in 1915. This store sells antique home furnishings, larger upholstery pieces, case goods, and wall art such as original oil paintings. This elegant old building provides a perfect setting for Mary Carol's selection of home furnishings.

Together these three stores offer a comprehensive selection of truly unique home furnishings merchandise that draws thousands of customers to Atchison every year. On a crisp autumn Tuesday, I stood behind Nell Hill's checkout and counted more than 200 shoppers, most of whom ended up buying something. Both of the other stores enjoy that kind of weekday traffic as well.

To accommodate the growing interest in her merchandise and fresh approach to home decor, Mary Carol recently opened a new 16,000-square-foot Nell Hill's store in Kansas City's Briarcliff Village. While the Atchison store has long attracted Kansas City customers, the new store will be even more convenient.

FRESH AND INTERESTING

Merchandise takes up every nook and cranny and packs shelves top to bottom. Customers marvel at the volume of treasures to explore in such a cozy atmosphere. If they can't find that perfect something the first time through the various sections of the store, they often go through again to make sure they haven't missed some treasure. But when they do find something they can't live without, they know to claim it right away because it might be gone when they go back.

Mary Carol's unusual merchandising philosophy adds to Nell Hill's charm. Rather than displaying similarly priced goods together, as is common in retail, inexpensive items sit alongside expensive ones, resulting in attractive presentations that add value to the inexpensive pieces. The sole goal is to create inviting displays with choices to fit every customer's budget and lifestyle. In this store, merchandise presentation is more about the style and overall look than about fitting a price point or pigeonholing an item into a particular category. This approach makes shopping in the store much more visually interesting and the merchandise more appealing.

The frequent remerchandising of whole sections of the store adds an element of surprise and keeps customers coming back again and again. Regularly weeding out slow sellers and integrating new items into the mix also keeps everything fresh and interesting. Shoppers never know what they will find from one visit to the next. Having visited there several times over the years, I am always astounded at just how much the store changes each time I stop by. It's not just the merchandise selection that changes; the walls in each room get painted different colors every year, giving the store a completely new look.

CHRISTMAS AT NELL HILL'S

The Christmas season, being the time of year when most retailers pull out all the stops, means stocking up on merchandise, sprucing up their stores, and determining how much discounting will have to be done to attract customers. Nell Hill's approach to the holiday season differentiates Mary Carol and her staff from other merchants. First, all year long she buys special merchandise specifically for the holidays. Second, to the delight of customers, Christmas goes into full swing by the end of August.

Prior to September 11, 2001, holiday merchandise displays went up in the first part of October, much like other retailers. Following the negative repercussions on the 2001 holiday season resulting from the horrors of 9/11, 2002 Christmas merchandise began to appear at Nell Hill's in the beginning of August. By the end of that month, the store was completely transformed into a holiday wonderland. After a year when so many people felt anxious and stressed out, introducing Christmas merchandise early at Nell Hill's was just what the doctor ordered.

Mary Carol found that the majority of her customers started planning home holiday decor as early as late summer. This early approach to seasonal products proved to be the perfect decision. Full-blown holiday selections in August are now a tradition that Nell Hill's customers expect to find. Those who don't visit the store early either don't get what they want or experience slim pickings later in the year.

Popular holiday attractions at Nell Hill's include a wondrous assortment of distinct and often one-of-a-kind Christmas tree ornaments. With a selection that isn't available elsewhere, customers come to the checkout counter toting as many filled baskets as they can carry in two hands. When customers can't take their purchases with them, Nell Hill's offers delivery to several communities within the region.

THE GUESTHOUSE

An interesting social phenomenon among female baby boomers began in the last few years. All across the country, small groups of women get together annually with their best high school or college friends and spend a few days together—no husbands or children allowed. Several years ago, Mary Carol, along with her husband/business partner, Dan, bought a lovely old Victorian-style house a few blocks from the store. They restored and decorated the house, transforming it into an exquisitely appointed yet comfortable guesthouse.

In a stroke of pure marketing genius, the Garritys now make their guesthouse available to these small groups of women as a destination for their annual reunions. Talking and reminiscing takes up a good portion of the time spent together, and the comfortable and private atmosphere of the guesthouse lends itself perfectly to the occasion. In addition to socializing, shopping seems to be a universally loved activity for these gatherings, and, as it turns out, they can find the very best stores in Atchison, Kansas—Nell Hill's, G. Diebolt's, and Garrity's Encore—only a few blocks away.

"ONE OF THE HOTTEST RETAILERS AROUND"

The first national media coverage for Nell Hill's, a front-page article in the *Wall Street Journal,* appeared back in 1997. While the original store (and the only one the Garritys operated at the time) already was successful and well known to customers in Kansas City and other nearby communities, that single *WSJ* article made the store a national destination, attracting a constant stream of new customers from all across the United States.

No amount of advertising could have accomplished what the *Wall Street Journal* article did for this single-store retailer. But that was just the beginning. Being one of the nation's best one-of-a-kind stores, Nell Hill's has since been featured in *Victoria* magazine, *Southern Living at Home, Midwest Living, Gifts & Decorative Accessories, Home Accents Today,* and dozens of daily newspapers. A recent issue of *Fortune* magazine referred to Mary Carol and her store as "one of the hottest retailers around."

PROMOTION AND BOOKS

The Garritys avoid most traditional advertising and come up with some creative alternatives to increase customer awareness and attract shoppers to the store. Being as popular as it is among Kansas City shoppers, Nell Hill's holds an annual Spring Open House, which se   every year. For a small fee, customers sign up for the event, b   bus in Kansas City, and are transported to Mary Carol's   n Atchison. There they enjoy a lovely lunch, take a tour of her   ully decorated home, and spend the rest of the day at Nell Hill's,   e they can shop to their heart's content. The Spring Open House   ginally started as a one-day event but became so popular that an   ditional day was added. Capitalizing on the attention the Spring   Open House generates, Mary Carol often introduces new merchandising lines to coincide with the open house. Recently she unveiled her own signature line of furniture, which includes sofas, ottomans, and upholstered chairs available in a wide variety of fabric choices.

In addition to the annual open house and other special events held throughout the year, an even more powerful marketing tool augments the mix. In 2001, Mary Carol's first book, *Nell Hill's Style at Home,* was published. This beautifully produced book, filled with photos, illustrates creative ideas to make one's home look better than it would had it been decorated by an ASID-certified interior designer. And more books followed: *Nell Hill's Christmas at Home* in 2003; *Nell Hill's Decorating Secrets: Easy and Inspiring Ways to Bring Style into Your*

Home in 2004; *Nell Hill's Entertaining in Style: Inspiring Parties and Seasonal Celebrations* in 2006; and, in 2007, *Nell Hill's Stylish Weddings* and *Nell Hill's Feather Your Nest: It's All in the Details.* One reason this series of books has enjoyed so much success is Mary Carol's innate ability to provide practical, usable decorating ideas and tips anyone can use in their home, whether a spacious colonial or a studio apartment. The books can be purchased in bookstores and through online booksellers.

To add to her growing fame and draw even more home furnishings customers to the stores, she writes a regular column on decorating that appears in the *Kansas City Star* as well as in a number of other daily newspapers around the country. Writing and publishing these wonderful books and articles further validates Nell Hill's and Mary Carol Garrity's place among America's top resources for decorating ideas and great home furnishings for everyone.

EXPANDING INFLUENCE

As one of the country's most important home furnishings and decor influencers, Mary Carol recently added a line of home accent pieces and custom paint colors to her offerings. These are now available in more than 750 stores across the country. The newest addition is a series of collector plates that she has been autographing at gift shows around the country.

While small-town retailers struggle to grow and even survive, Mary Carol proves it doesn't really matter where a retailer is located or how small the town. If they give customers enough compelling reasons to get into their cars and drive to the store, they will. For nearly thirty years Mary Carol Garrity has been attracting customers to her store with very little advertising and an unconventional approach to doing business.

The combination of a great store, merchandise that appeals to a wide range of consumers, exclusive product lines, bestselling decorating books, a widely read newspaper column, and lots of special events

with jeans and an open-collar shirt left untucked. LouisBoston freely mixes merchandise styles and designers.

Customers notice the changes in the store the moment they walk through the door. The first-floor merchandise mix supports Debi's more lifestyle-oriented merchandising theme. Their buying options are no longer exclusively apparel. Customers can buy exquisite bed and bath linen, soaps and lotions, home decor accessories, packaged gourmet foods, and music CDs at the bar behind which a DJ plays music on weekends. Everything lives up to the standards of excellence expected in LouisBoston, including the superb art hanging on the walls.

Long known for its extraordinary commitment to quality and fashionable menswear, LouisBoston's expansion of the Women's Apparel and Shoe departments can be attributed to Debi Greenberg's foresight. Women no longer come in to LouisBoston to shop solely for the men in their lives; they have plenty of reasons to shop for themselves. Today, women's apparel, accessories, and shoes account for as much as 40 percent of the inventory.

The circular dressing room area makes up the centerpiece of LouisBoston's Women's Apparel Department located on the top floor. Created by well-known retail designer Tim Button, this comfortable yet stylish space provides a center seating area that allows women shopping together to relax, chat, and show each other what they are trying on.

LouisBoston's once-a-year clearance sale takes place in January. Being the only sale LouisBoston holds throughout the year, it has become the preeminent event for anyone in quest of great buys on better-quality apparel. The promise of high-quality, fashionable merchandise at half price draws huge crowds and attracts significant media attention in Boston. In 2007 an article appeared in *Boston Magazine,* and was posted on its Web site, that provided a strategy to prospective customers for shopping the LouisBoston sale. Some of the tips included: "Scope out the store beforehand and try on pieces that catch your eye. Plan to arrive by 9:00 a.m.; the store opens at 10:00 a.m.

Take a taxi since the store's lot only holds 40 cars. Don't bother hunting down salesclerks to check in the back for other sizes. If it's not out
on the floor, you're out of luck. Take the stairs since the elevators are
small and slower." What store wouldn't love to have this kind of free
publicity for its annual sale?

ARCHITECTURALLY DYNAMIC

Great architecture has long been a hallmark of retail landmarks
across the country. New York boasts Bloomingdale's and Saks Fifth
Avenue. Trendy retailer Forever 21 recently moved into an architecturally dynamic building on San Francisco's Powell Street, preserving
the classic features and tall ceilings within the building. LouisBoston,
located on the corner of Berkeley Street and Boston's famous Newbury
Street, occupies the original New England Museum of Natural
History building built in 1863. At 40,000 square feet on four floors,
it is one of the most beautiful and interesting retail spaces in the
country. Prior to LouisBoston's moving into the building in 1989, it
housed a Bonwit Teller store. The tall ceilings, beautiful wood floors,
elegant staircase, and classic architecture highlight the impressively
displayed merchandise.

There is more to this great retail destination than its exceptional
selection of fashionable apparel, shoes, accessories, and other merchandise. On the first floor of the store, the Morgenthal Frederics
EyeGlass Department sells some very cool eyewear designs. The
Mario Russo hair salon, Boston's premier salon, shares space in the
building, as does Boston Public, a steak house with Asian influences
that has become very popular with Bostonians and tourists alike.
While separate from LouisBoston and having their own entrances, all
three businesses benefit from one another's popularity with selective
clientele.

At one time the Newbury Street area was a haven for upscale retailers, art galleries, and fine dining. The neighborhood no longer
carries that air of sophisticated exclusivity and has become home to a

number of mass merchants, including H&M, Victoria's Secret, and Filene's Basement, as well as several mid-tier restaurants. Because of this change in environment, LouisBoston recently announced it will likely move to a new location when its lease is up in the next few years. Being a destination store, its upscale customers surely will follow it.

Debi takes a bold, pioneering approach to LouisBoston's inventory, how the store looks, and customer service. Murray Pearlstein taught his daughter well. She's just as opinionated, gutsy, and unafraid to move the business forward as was her father. "Product is our number one force, that's where we put our focus," Debi points out. "We want customers to discover and find new things they've not seen before." LouisBoston has always been ahead of the curve when it comes to store design and merchandise selection. Few apparel stores can better meet the needs of the northeastern chic.

As LouisBoston shows every day, there will always be opportunities in the retail marketplace for innovative merchants. Meanwhile, imitators will be left in the dust scrapping for customers.

LouisBoston
234 Berkeley Street
Boston, Massachusetts 02116
(617) 262-6100
www.louisboston.com

More photos of LouisBoston can be seen at
www.retailsuperstars.com/louisboston.

Estes Ark

Travelers driving toward the small, scenic Rocky Mountain community of Estes Park, Colorado, will discover an ark sitting alongside Highway 34 at the city limits. Unlike Noah's famous vessel, this ark won't float, but it is home to thousands of animals—the stuffed variety—representing almost all those that survived on that biblical ark.

BUILDING AN ARK

In 1984, Susan and Steve Swickard opened The Talking Teddy, a 900-square-foot shop on the main street of downtown Estes Park. Named for a talking toy bear from the 1950s, this little store epitomized the Swickards' love of teddy bears. Several years and two moves later, the couple's ever increasing inventory of teddy bears and other stuffed animals demanded more space. But they envisioned something different from simply a larger store. What better place could be built to house stuffed animals than an ark?

Designing a memorable, truly one-of-a-kind structure will differentiate a retailer from the competition right off the bat. Such a structure may initially be more costly, but the buzz it creates can mean spending less on marketing campaigns. Stores like the original Bass Pro Shop in Springfield, Missouri; Nebraska Furniture Mart in Kansas City, Kansas; and the Crate & Barrel on Chicago's Michigan Avenue all have successfully used bold architecture to capture the attention of consumers.

In the early 1990s, the Swickards bought a parcel of land overlooking Lake Estes on the highway leading into town and commenced construction. Building their ark presented plenty of challenges, starting with finding a construction crew appropriately skilled to take on this architectural endeavor. Among the many skills to master was just how far one could bend twenty-foot-long two-by-fours to create the boat's hull. Following several failed attempts and much experimentation, the construction crew eventually determined the right combination of water needed to soften the wood and perfect the bending procedure. Two years later, after a great deal of hard work, the ark was completed. In November of 1995, Estes Ark opened to the public.

At 100 feet long, 50 feet wide, and 30 feet tall, this unusual boat-shaped structure guarantees catching the attention of anyone passing by. As architecturally correct as one can gather from the Bible story, the completed Estes Ark measured approximately one quarter the size of the biblical ark. Local building codes, rather than biblical blueprints, dictated how Estes Ark was to be built. The ark appears to be floating in a pond. To enter it, visitors must traverse a 25-foot ramp. The ramp leads to a walkway surrounding the structure, taking customers through an 8-foot-square main floor entrance.

Three floors of merchandise covering 5,000 square feet and over 10,000 animals on board visually delight children and adults alike. The nautical theme carries throughout each level of the ark, with merchandise presented creatively. Using wooden barrels for lighting, ropes as netting, and cubbyholes, stairways, and webbed ropes for displays, the entire structure feels much like what one might imagine an ancient ark to be.

As the popularity of plush toys has increased, so has Estes Ark's status as a destination for visitors to this busy tourist area. Since its restructuring in 1995, Estes Ark has been widely recognized by the retail and gift industry press. The store has received many awards, such as "Specialty Retailer of the Year," "Best Store Design," "Outstanding Display and Product Representation," "Best Direct Merchandising," and "Outstanding Retail Display." But the most important recognition of all comes from the legions of customers who shop in this wonderful store year after year.

TEDDY BEARS LIVE ON THE MAIN FLOOR

A wonderful assortment of teddy bears, the store's mainstay, take up residence on the main floor. Shoppers exploring this teddy bear sanctuary find a bounty of bears and bear accessories—from the smallest miniatures to such popular brands as Steiff, Gund, Douglas, and the Muffy VanderBear collection. Celebrity bear sightings reveal some "Very Important Bears" such as Bearilyn Monroe, Scarlett O'Beara, and Libearace, plus a special area devoted to the famous firefighter Smokey Bear. Unlike the wild variety, these bears wear clothes. Apparel shoppers can find a wide assortment of dresses, pajamas, swimsuits, uniforms, and overalls to fill out their teddy bear's closet.

Not all are toys. Vintage teddy bears are displayed throughout, along with an adorable selection of bear figurines. Some rare and desirable collectibles live here as well and can cost hundreds of dollars.

NOAH'S ATTIC

One floor up, Noah's Attic showcases ark-themed merchandise, including several toy arks in various sizes, materials, and price ranges. One even floats on the water, has a working crane and cages in the hull, and comes with several pairs of animals along with Noah and Mrs. Noah. Noah the Creature Teacher, an educational game for young children that can be expanded as they grow, teaches the names of the animals and their spellings. More games, collectibles, clothing, puzzles, lamps, CDs, DVDs, and books can be purchased, along with several plush animals paired male and female as they would have been entering the ark two by two. Only these pairs wear ribbons—a bow around the neck of the male and on the head of the female. Exclusive cubit rulers add to the Noah's Ark theme. (The cubit, an ancient unit of measure, is said to equal the length of a man's arm from elbow to the end of the middle finger, or no less than 18 inches, although some may argue it measures from the elbow to the base of the hand, or 12 inches. In the biblical story of Noah, the cubit was the measure used in God's size specifications for building the ark— 300 cubits long, 50 cubits wide, and 30 cubits high.)

THE ANIMALS LIVING UP TOP

The ark's third and uppermost level houses a wide variety of domestic and exotic stuffed animals displayed by species. Some live in stalls and others hang from the ceiling. The largest sit on shelves around the upper reaches of the structure. That such an extensive array of plush critters can be gathered together in one place astounds customers. Many of the stuffed or plush animals appear startlingly authentic; others are just plain cute. On this floor customers can delight in all the animals that survived on Noah's Ark.

Here is a smattering of the creatures, some in the form of puppets, that live on the third floor: armadillo, bat, camel, condor, echidna, flamingo, gorilla, hippopotamus, horseshoe crab, jellyfish, kudu, lizard, lobster, naked mole rat, octopus, okapi, ostrich, platypus, rainbow trout, rhinoceros, ring-tailed lemur and other lemur varieties, roadrunner, scorpion, sea turtle, sloth, tarantula, toucan, tropical fish, whale, and wolverine.

THE BELLY OF THE SHIP

The lowest level, or belly, of the ship houses the offices, merchandising storage, and the Rainbow Room. Originally this room was used for seminars, community events, and special appearances by designers, but in 2005 the Rainbow Room was transformed into a blast from the past. "The Rainbow Curve Slot Car Raceway recaptures the experience of a 1960s style slot car raceway with a six-lane, 100-foot, custom-built wooden track," Susan remarks. "Nostalgic fun for the entire family—perfect play for a rainy day."

Building the slot car raceway feeds the resurgence of this competitive hobby and draws customers into the store. The longer a retailer can keep customers in the store, the more likely they are to buy something. With an added attraction like the Rainbow Curve Slot Car Raceway, the odds are pretty good that customers will want to spend even more time at Estes Ark.

CELEBRATING TEDDY BEARS

Every year for the last twenty-four, Estes Ark hosts a major special event—the Teddy Bear Picnic. The musical theme of this annual celebration dates back to the early years of the last century. In 1907, composer John W. Bratton wrote "The Teddy Bears' Picnic," and in 1932, Irish lyricist Jimmy Kennedy added words. The song, widely played on the BBC, didn't achieve real popularity in the United States until it was used as the theme for *Big Jon and Sparkie,* a well-known children's radio program from the late 1940s and 1950s. Kids growing up during those years, before television captured their attention, often remember hearing that song on the radio virtually every Saturday morning.

Estes Ark's Teddy Bear Picnic draws hundreds of visitors to the store each year. This popular charity fund-raiser truly celebrates teddy bears and has featured such famous celebrities as Winnie-the-Pooh, Corduroy, Yogi, Boo Boo, Paddington, and Cindy Bear. Kids eagerly participate in the teddy bear coloring contest. Prizes are awarded for the largest teddy bear and the smallest teddy bear. "Even the A&W Root Bear has served up his famous treats to round out this free family event," adds Susan with a smile.

Some years allow for additional celebrations and events. The event celebrating the hundredth anniversary of the teddy bear attracted teddy bear lovers and collectors from all across the country. Bruce Raiffe, president of Gund, America's oldest stuffed toy company, made a special appearance. Smokey Bear's fiftieth birthday party added educational fun and allowed Smokey to spread his message of fire safety.

Maxine Clark's successful Build-A-Bear Workshop chain proves positive the appeal of teddy bears to both adults and children. Susan and Steve Swickard have built this incredible business around teddy bears, the animals of Noah's Ark, plus some creatures that don't fit into either category. Hundreds of stores may sell stuffed animals, but only one exists where customers can shop for and see all these animals in an actual ark. To build such a store takes great vision, commitment, and the desire to stand out in a retail marketplace filled with ordinary look-alikes.

CUSTOMER-FRIENDLY WEB SITE

The Talking Teddy produced a homespun catalog from 1985 to 1997. Now, Estes Ark augments its business through Internet sales. The creatively designed Web site holds true to the ark theme. Categories for specific types of merchandise and animal species can easily be navigated by online visitors.

Customers who can't get into the store to touch and feel the merchandise firsthand will enjoy wandering through Estesark.com. Its excellently photographed likenesses of all the items and succinct descriptions, which include size and materials used, give collectors and toy lovers the world over a clear understanding of what they're about to buy. It's refreshing to experience a Web site that organizes the shopping process from a customer's point of view.

AN IMPORTANT PART OF THE TOY INDUSTRY

Some segments of the toy business have struggled in recent years due to the increased prevalence of electronic games. But the plush toy segment continues to grow and expand year after year. Beanie Babies, among the most popular toys of all time, sold in the millions. Close on the heels of Beanie Babies came Webkinz, a plush line that encourages buyers to go online, learn more about their toys, interact with other buyers, and, of course, buy more Webkinz toys and accessories.

Undoubtedly another hot new toy will burst upon the scene, but teddy bears and other soft, cuddly stuffed animals will continue to claim a special place in the hearts of our children. After all, American kids have long considered their teddy bears to be their first best friend and have done so since 1902. Electronic games will never usurp the teddy bear.

The uniqueness of Estes Ark stands out and grabs attention. Customers marvel at visiting all those creatures living in Noah's Ark.

This is not just one of America's best stores—it ranks among the great architectural achievements for a retail store anywhere in the world.

Estes Ark

521 Lone Pine Drive

Estes Park, Colorado 80517

(970) 586-6483

WWW.ESTESARK.COM

More photos of Estes Ark can be seen at

WWW.RETAILSUPERSTARS.COM/ESTESARK.

Junkman's Daughter

Siblings Pam Majors and Mark Gavron—children of "The Junkman"—created Junkman's Daughter and Junkman's Daughter's Brother, repectively. The store names immediately grab the attention of potential customers and reflect the uniqueness of the stores themselves. Everything about these stores is fun—from the offbeat and sometimes provocative merchandise to the stimulating upbeat colors and fuzzy, furry, glittery decor throughout.

IT STARTED WITH BIG G SURPLUS

Years ago in Atlanta, Georgia, Edwin Gavron built a successful salvage business—Big G Surplus—by buying and selling new, closeout, distressed, and dead stock. "My mother, Ruth, was stuck running the store while Dad had the fun of running around looking for deals or playing cards in a warehouse with the other salvage dealers," recalls Pam Majors. "A lot of deals were bought and sold around that card table."

When Edwin Gavron decided it was time to retire, he had over forty years of accumulated merchandise to dispose of before he could close the store. Pam helped him sort through and figure out what to do with all these things. Some of the stuff certainly was junk, but there were plenty of highly desirable and quite saleable goods as well.

During this painstaking process, Pam uncovered some amazing treasures hidden away in the nooks and crannies of the Big G Surplus building. Among the most prized of these treasures were such things as unopened boxes of Mickey Mouse toys from the 1950s and '60s, original boxes of nylon stockings marked "1942," Beatles notebooks from the 1960s, and a box of battery-operated toy Coca-Cola trucks. Some years before, one of her father's purchases had been some small toy trucks from the Coca-Cola Company. He bought the trucks for 10 cents each. During her discovery Pam found a full box of the highly desirable toy trucks that had been overlooked.

Pam gathered the best merchandise from her father's collections and in 1982 opened her own store. To honor her father, she named her store Junkman's Daughter. "Dad was never called the Junkman," Pam reminisces, "but he loved the name of the store." And by the way, "I kept the Coca-Cola trucks," she says smiling. "I think they list for over $750 now."

JUNKMAN'S DAUGHTER

Junkman's Daughter started out in a small, 1,000-square-foot space in an area of Atlanta called Little Five Points. Little Five Points, long known as one of Atlanta's oldest and quirkiest neighborhoods, and particularly desirable for independent retailers, proved the perfect place for such a store. The area was in the midst of a revitalization from a run-down neighborhood with older stores, many vacant, that had been there for years. "As in most cities, revitalization came with artists and students looking for affordable housing who pioneered a move to the area," Pam explains. "I was among this group buying a house in 1976 for $29,000. The homes are now $400,000 to $800,000."

Over the next few years, Pam's business grew and she moved several times into larger and larger spaces, always in the same neighborhood. With each move she expanded her assortment of offbeat merchandise. Junkman's Daughter became a favorite hangout for local teenagers. "Even the first store was a hangout," she recalls. "We always listened to the kids and tried to get what they wanted." By the early 1990s the Little Five Points area had established itself nationally as an alternative urban shopping district with unique small stores and restaurants.

During one period of time, Pam owned and managed two locations across the street from each other, the second of which was called Princess Pamela's Tchotchke Palace, managed by her son, Josh Mills. But in 1993, she merged her two stores and moved into the 10,000-square-foot building she bought on Moreland Avenue, where Junkman's Daughter can be found today. In one of those strangely ironic parallels that happens sometimes, the building Pam bought had formerly been a supermarket, as was the building her father had purchased long ago for Big G Surplus.

The area surrounding Little Five Points inevitably changed, and today the Eaglewood Shopping District, one neighborhood south, includes such national chain stores as Office Depot, Target, Best Buy, and the usual Starbucks. But the immediate area around Junkman's

Daughter remains a unique mix of quirky stores, restaurants, and people.

WHAT KIND OF STORE IS THIS?

It's tough to describe Junkman's Daughter because it's unlike any other, except maybe Junkman's Daughter's Brother, which is detailed in the next chapter. At 10,000 square feet, it can hardly be classified as a boutique, yet it feels smaller and more intimate than most stores of this size. To use Pam's own words, the store is "entertaining, outrageous, and affordable." She's absolutely right. The merchandise might be described by some as outrageous, a little bawdy, or even shocking, but it definitely entertains and certainly is affordable.

In general terms, the store's various departments can be categorized as apparel, gifts, shoes, posters, art, jewelry, household goods, costumes, and a selection of smoking paraphernalia. More specifically, the store offers a diversified mix of contemporary and vintage apparel that will appeal to anyone wishing to use clothing to make a statement. Wigs, on display throughout the extensive Apparel Department, come in a multitude of provocative styles and colors—from orange to shocking pink. Lingerie, also prominently displayed, can be worn either under another garment or all by itself, as fashion dictates.

Customers looking for something sedate, staid, or conservative won't find it here. On the other hand, anyone looking for trendy apparel on the cutting edge of fashion will discover a satisfying assortment at Junkman's Daughter.

JAW-DROPPING OUT-OF-THIS-WORLD SHOES

The stairway up to the Shoe Department has been built to look like a giant, red high-heeled shoe that spans the full twenty-foot height of the staircase. Once upstairs in the Shoe Department loft, women can choose from platform shoes that will add eighteen inches to their height; glitter-covered footwear in shades from the brightest pinks to the richest reds; thigh-high, stiletto-heeled leather boots; sneakers in a rainbow of colors; and sexy sling-backs for an evening of club hopping. And for aspiring clowns, a fine selection of those cool-looking, colorful, oversize shoes worn by circus clowns awaits. Even if shoes aren't on the shopping list, it's worth climbing up the stairs to see the view of the store from the loft.

AND COSTUMES

Every bit a major holiday to the Little Five Points residents and businesses, Halloween includes an annual festival featuring a parade with floats. Everyone dresses up and parties in the streets. Junkman's Daughter rearranges the store at this time of year to accommodate its considerable selection of costumes, masks, and facial transformation products (makeup, fake beards, gross-looking rubber scars, blood, and gore). A customer can find a few costumes and masks year-round, but at Halloween this department takes on a life of its own.

HOBNOB WITH THE STARS

With its Little Five Points location and a reputation among fashion mavens for unique merchandise, Junkman's Daughter attracts its share of celebrities, movie stars, and musicians. You might find yourself rubbing elbows with Brad Pitt, Kevin Costner, Courtney Love, Alanis Morissette, or Alice Cooper, and maybe musicians from such bands as U2 and ZZ Top.

This store is FUN! The merchandise itself, the employees, the various props around the store, and even the signage all make it a joyful place to shop. If you've been alive for more than forty years and your life has been somewhat sheltered, you may be a little shocked by some of the things you will see. But, no matter how young or old or sheltered you are or whether you're interested or not in owning a bright pink wig or a pair of thigh-high leather boots, you will enjoy a few laughs in this store.

As a longtime advocate of the importance for retailers to create distinguishable stores, I applaud Pam Majors for doing just that. As long as she offers distinctive merchandise and a zany store environment, she will enjoy success. It is a way of doing business that not everyone is capable of mastering. With more than twenty-five years in business, she gets it.

Junkman's Daughter
464 Moreland Avenue NE
Atlanta, Georgia 30307
(404) 577-3188

More photos of Junkman's Daughter can be seen at
www.retailsuperstars.com/junkmansdaughter.

Junkman's Daughter's Brother

Athens, Georgia

Throughout the early part of Mark Gavron's working career, it never occurred to him that he would end up in retail. Looking back, though, he now realizes it was in his blood. After graduating from the University of Georgia, he spent several years as a working geologist. When the oil business turned down in the early 1980s, Mark knew it was time for a career change. He saw what a kick his sister was having with Junkman's Daughter and decided to join in.

Not wanting the new store to compete with Pam's original store or take away from it in any way, Mark and Pam opened a store near the University of Georgia in Athens to serve the student population. And so in 1986, Junkman's Daughter's Brother came to be. Laughingly, Mark tells of another store he ran for a while, called Junkman's Other Daughter's Brother, "who, of course, is me." It isn't around anymore. Probably a good thing; this can get confusing,

When it comes to remembering the names, one may not get it exactly right, but nobody will likely forget Junkman's Daughter and Junkman's Daughter's Brother once they've been there for a visit. Some similarities exist between the two, but also significant differences. Junkman's Daughter, because it is located in a big-city neighborhood with a population of younger working adults as well as students, can offer merchandise at higher price points that satisfy the tastes of the store's diverse, urban customer base.

Junkman's Daughter's Brother serves a much different customer—mostly university students on limited budgets. So generally the store carries inexpensive merchandise, with few items priced over $100. But the more than 30,000 students who live on and around the Athens campus provide an extraordinary business opportunity for a savvy merchant like Mark Gavron.

WHAT KIND OF STUFF DO THEY SELL?

The merchandise selection in the first incarnation of Junkman's Daughter's Brother, located in a 2,000-square-foot space in downtown Athens, was limited to trendy and vintage clothing, jewelry, and some toys. As the business grew, Mark moved the store to a larger building, allowing him to add posters and T-shirts and an expanded selection of toys, clothing, and jewelry.

The current location measures 12,000 square feet on two floors and offers a massive amount of merchandise. A selection of posters that students can use to cover the walls of their dorm rooms is among the staples, with more than 1,400 different titles. A student looking for something unusual or out of the ordinary will not be disappointed. But dorm room decor extends beyond posters. Inexpensive bedspreads, beaded curtains, room dividers, and humorous doormats, all available in choices of styles and colors, complete the look.

Lava lamps, cards, books, balloons, clocks, wind chimes, picture frames, the all-important barware college students need for in-room entertaining, and cookie jars in the most bizarre shapes and sizes fill the shelves. An authentic reproduction of a 1956 Corvette—bright red with the white stripe on the side—was just one of the cookie jar choices. And then there's the most humongous selection of PEZ dispensers you're likely to see anywhere. The smoking section can be found upstairs for those who enjoy tobacco and other kinds of herbs requiring assorted paraphernalia.

College students, whose apparel preferences consist mostly of T-shirts and a pair of shorts or jeans, will find a massive T-shirt selection in the Athens store. The mix constantly changes, but there are always between 600 and 700 different styles from which to choose. "There's no reason for anyone to go anywhere else for posters or T-shirts," Mark says, "because we have the best selection." A student can spend hours in the store and still not see the entire collection.

Beyond posters and T-shirts, the Clothing and Jewelry departments in the back of the store offer a wide range of trendy and vintage apparel, wigs, jewelry, and purses. The customer looking for anything from military-style jackets to vintage formal dresses to funky fur coats will surely find just the right thing. And if one needs black or dark purple nail polish and lipstick to finish off the Goth look, that's there, too. "The girls come in for clothing and drag their boyfriends in," Mark laughs. "While the girls shop for clothes the guys do something completely different." With all there is to see, the guys can entertain themselves for hours exploring the store and its diverse selection of merchandise.

HALLOWEEN

While on the topic of creating a "look," the Costume Rental Department, located upstairs, is like a store unto itself. Fraternity and sorority costume parties keep this department busy all year long. But Halloween takes the prize. October at Junkman's Daughter's Brother rivals Christmas in most other retail stores. For two weeks leading up to Halloween, it's absolute chaos.

"WE BUY STUFF WE LIKE"

The store's staff of sixteen to eighteen mostly full-time employees can handle even the busiest days with ease. One of the things that makes this store notable from a business standpoint is that department managers do the buying for their own departments, contrary to how it's traditionally done in larger retail companies. When asked how they decide what to buy for the store, Mark says, "We buy stuff we like." It doesn't hurt that the managers/buyers all have worked in the store for years and know what their customers will buy. In many retail businesses the buying process is tedious and boring. For Mark and his buyers, it is always fun and a great adventure looking for things that will thrill their customers.

When Mark and the buyers attend trade shows in Atlanta and elsewhere, they scour the place looking for out-of-the-ordinary and provocative items that will get their customers excited. While not everything they buy sells immediately, the variety adds to the "treasure hunt" experience their customers enjoy.

National chain retailers have come to realize the important role music plays in shaping a customer's shopping experience. The music selection at Junkman's Daughter's Brother suits the alternative bent of everything else in the store. On most days the staff brings in their own favorites, so the diversity of artists and musical styles enhances the cheeky feeling.

TWO STORES TO DELIGHT

There isn't a retailer alive who doesn't want customers to passionately love shopping in their stores. By offering highly focused selections of merchandise that appeal to a distinct group of customers, Pam and Mark have created stores in which customers passionately love to shop. Years of steady growth attest to the ability of these two merchants to sustain successful retail enterprises.

Because of the posters, T-shirts, beaded door curtains, and smoking supplies being sold, one might want to compare these stores to the "head shops" of the 1960s. That would be a mistake. The merchandise and decor may be geared more toward younger consumers, but the selection in both stores is eccentric, interesting, and contemporary enough to intrigue everyone.

"I think the joy of it for Mark and myself is the treasure hunting," Pam concludes. "We definitely got this from our father and I think we've made him proud."

JUNKMAN'S DAUGHTER'S BROTHER

458 E. CLAYTON STREET

ATHENS, GEORGIA 30601

(706) 543-4454

MORE PHOTOS OF JUNKMAN'S DAUGHTER'S BROTHER

CAN BE SEEN AT

WWW.RETAILSUPERSTARS.COM/JUNKMANSDB.

Smoky Mountain Knife Works

Sevierville, Tennessee

In the fall of 2004, on a flight from New York City to Boston, my seatmate asked what brought me to Boston. I explained I was writing a book about one-of-a-kind stores and was on my way to see a store I was considering for the book. He immediately grabbed his briefcase, pulled out a copy of a knife magazine, and enthusiastically proclaimed, "Here's a store that would be great for your book. You have to go see it!" The magazine featured an article on Smoky Mountain Knife Works. He was right; I just had to see this store.

In this book filled with one-of-a-kind stores, Smoky Mountain Knife Works is one of the most unusual and innovative of them all. This extremely successful retail enterprise, owned by Kevin Pipes, lies in the foothills of eastern Tennessee, home to Smoky Mountain National Park. A popular tourist attraction in its own right, Smoky Mountain Knife Works welcomes as many as 1.2 million visitors annually.

A CONVERTED HOUSE

In 1978, spurred by their mutual interest in Indian artifacts, Kevin Pipes and John Parker started buying and selling collectible arrowheads and other such relics. Like many budding entrepreneurs, their first transactions took place at local flea markets. For some who want to get into business for themselves, selling at flea markets, swap meets, other outdoor markets, and even eBay provides an excellent, low-cost way to start. While they operated their weekend business, the partners continued to work at other jobs because their young enterprise did not yet provide a sufficient living for them to depend on it full-time. Kevin was in real estate and John worked for a printer. In the course of conducting his real estate business, Kevin came upon an old house in Pigeon Forge, Tennessee, in an area that recently had been zoned for commercial use. He knew it would be the perfect setting for their Indian artifact business. This former private residence became the original Smoky Mountain Knife Works.

As they were getting ready to open the new store, John's brother offered to supply pocketknives for inclusion in their inventory. Knowing their resources were limited, he provided the knives on consignment. Doubtful at the time, Kevin thought, "Nobody buys pocketknives." Reluctantly, he agreed to display them. As it turned out, very few customers bought Indian artifacts, but they did, indeed, buy lots of pocketknives. The partners had found their niche.

Eventually John left the business, which is now wholly owned by Kevin. In 1991 Kevin oversaw the construction of the building they currently occupy in Sevierville. The original plan was to house both the warehouse and the store under one roof, but before long the store proved to be the driving force. In need of more retail space, Kevin moved the warehouse into its own building. At that time the store covered 55,000 square feet on two levels. The business continued to grow and, bursting at the seams, it expanded further. In early 2005 an addition of 28,000 square feet was built, increasing the store's total square footage to 83,000 on three levels, with parking all around the outside.

THE WORLD'S LARGEST KNIFE SHOWPLACE

With knives being one of the oldest and most useful tools known to man, the number of collectible and usable varieties seems endless. A store would have to have a huge selection to attract more than a million customers there each year. The collection at Smoky Mountain Knife Works does just that, showing every conceivable type of knife.

Multi- and single-bladed pocketknives come as small as two inches to as large as six inches when closed. Customers can peruse thousands of usable varieties as well as a wide assortment commemorating such historical events as World War II, the Korean and Vietnam wars, and Iraqi Freedom, plus knives from popular movies such as the Rambo series. Victorinox Swiss army knives can be purchased in a number of places, but Smoky Mountain Knife Works carries the entire line from the single-blade Solo to the Master Gardener and Master Electrician models, with every blade or tool one could possibly want.

Several versions of the famous Bowie knife serve hunting and fishing enthusiasts. Sheaf knives, machetes, stilettos, daggers, throwing knives, framelocks, and even the current U.S. Marine Corps combat utility bayonet add to the selection. The tremendous representation of brands includes Browning, Buck Knives, Case, Cold Steel, Columbia River, Falcon, Frost Cutlery, Gerber, Hen & Rooster,

Kershaw, Marbel's Outdoors, Remington, Robeson-MasterCraft, Rough Rider, Schrade, Smith & Wesson, and Winchester. Logo branded knives also come from such well-known brands as Harley-Davidson and Ford.

While knives hold the primary focus, the store also stocks reproductions of military swords such as German, Scottish, Japanese, and the U.S. Navy cutlass, plus replicas from ancient times and from such movies as *The Lord of the Rings* and *Pirates of the Caribbean.* In addition to fantasy swords, a number of fantasy knives can be found with sweeping blades and intricate handles.

MORE THAN A MAN'S STORE

The first floor houses Smoky Mountain Kitchen Works, showing a comprehensive selection of kitchen knives, tools, and cooking accessories. While the "Knife Works" portion of the store primarily attracts men (although not exclusively), "Kitchen Works" delights anyone who has an interest in cooking.

The enormous number of knives, swords, and cutlery certainly dominates the store, but Kevin doesn't devote all the space to displaying and selling merchandise. Customers enjoy browsing showcases filled with antique and rare knives going back to the 1700s as well as mounted great game animals, a giant two-story sword in the stone, and an impressive waterfall. Throughout the store men, women, and children can view exhibits celebrating our country's history, including the weapons and tools that shaped America.

In November of 2006, the National Knife Museum opened inside Smoky Mountain Knife Works in a section donated by Kevin. The museum occupies 4,500 square feet, allowing the National Knife Collectors Association to showcase its extensive array of knives from throughout history. Formerly housed in rented space in Chattanooga, the organization's collection of more than 12,000 knives has found the perfect home.

A POPULAR TOURIST DESTINATION

The Smoky Mountain Knife Works locale draws tourists to such year-round attractions as Great Smoky Mountains National Park; Dollywood, country music star Dolly Parton's theme park; and several large outlet shopping centers. When the trees begin to change in the fall, traffic in and out of the area crawls while people take in nature at its most colorful.

In an area of the country where hunting, fishing, and camping rank high among favored pastimes, Smoky Mountain Knife Works attracts both collectors and outdoor sports enthusiasts. Combine that with its great location on the same highway that leads to the popular national park, a creative approach to catalog and Internet marketing, and even its own television program, it's no wonder Smoky Mountain Knife Works brings in so many visitors year after year.

REACHING THE WORLD

Narrowly defined specialty retailers have long used catalogs to spread the word and stay in touch with customers. Smoky Mountain Knife Works uses this medium to the fullest. Its catalog of over 100 pages currently goes out to no fewer than five million knife, sword, and kitchenware buyers annually.

The easy-to-navigate, quick-loading Web site (Smokymountain knifeworks.com) allows access to much of the store's merchandise, and in some instances displays an even wider selection than what's available in the store. Knives, swords, axes, sharpeners, kitchen gadgets, cigarette lighters, camping and fishing equipment, martial arts weapons, flashlights, books, and even jams, jellies, preserves, and fruit butters can be purchased online. Visitors can also view the current and upcoming catalogs, clearance items, and Smoky Mountain Knife Works exclusives designed by Kevin and his senior designer, Brian Wilholte.

Smoky Mountain Knife Works broadcasts its own TV show on the DISH Network and DirecTV, and has proven to be one of the company's most effective marketing tools. *KnivesLIVE Home Shopping,* in its fourth year of production, broadcasts from a studio located in the same building as the store. The Monday and Friday evening shows, hosted by Steve Koontz, Tony Watkins, and Jay Parker, feature exclusive Smoky Mountain Knife Works merchandise and are produced by Kevin Pipes's own Smokey Mountain Network. Few retailers are willing or able to produce and broadcast their own TV show, but *KnivesLIVE* is a highly successful revenue generator for Smoky Mountain Knife Works, representing a reported 20 percent of the company's overall business.

THE IMPORTANCE OF A STERLING REPUTATION

The Internet provides a means for consumers to check out whether a particular product is what it claims to be and whether it is worth buying. Consumers can also check out a store to make sure it is a reputable place to shop and stands behind the merchandise it sells. These widely used peer-to-peer Web sites help consumers make informed buying decisions.

On a recent visit to one such peer-to-peer Web site, I found this question: "Anybody bought from Smoky Mountain Knife Works?" Here is a sampling of the universal praise from respondents. "Good people with good prices." "Many times. It's also a great place to visit if you're ever in their neck of the woods." "Buy with confidence. No worries." "I've bought from both the catalog and the Web site. I have always been satisfied." "I absolutely love that store, super great people who know their stuff." The guy who originally posted the question answered with this: "Thanks guys, I'm gonna have to blow some money here."

ONE OF THE GOOD GUYS

Back in the early days of the Iraq war, Kevin Pipes learned that our soldiers needed knives. So he initiated the program "A Knife for a Soldier" and helped collect funds from customers to buy knives for our troops fighting in Iraq. He negotiated with several of his suppliers to provide knives at special prices and even some at no cost. Kevin also convinced United Parcel Service to donate the shipping. Several thousand American soldiers in Iraq have been thrilled to receive the knives, all because a retailer in Tennessee took the initiative to do something good for soldiers fighting in a land far away from home. The program continues, nearing its goal of putting 10,000 knives in our soldiers' hands.

As retailers respond to and deal with the ups and downs of the economy, changing levels of consumer confidence, fierce competition, and even changes in the political climate, they must take bold steps to reach out and serve consumers. There's little doubt that staking a claim to a narrow, well-defined specialty category makes an effective strategy for growing a business. By coupling such a strategy with innovative marketing tools and excellent day-to-day business practices, you get the likes of Smoky Mountain Knife Works. I have no doubt that Kevin Pipes and his wonderful store will continue to enjoy long-term success.

Smoky Mountain Knife Works
2320 Winfield Dunn Parkway
Sevierville, Tennessee 37876
(865) 453-5871
www.smokymountainknifeworks.com

More photos of Smoky Mountain Knife Works can be seen at www.retailsuperstars.com/smokymountain.

Bering's

Independent retailers doing business in cities as large as

Houston often struggle to distinguish their stores from the competition—a major challenge in so competitive a marketplace. Bering's stands up to the challenge by targeting its merchandise and services to the affluent consumers living in its immediate community. Such a task takes a whole new way of thinking by those at the helm of what was once a traditional hardware store and home center.

National home center chains can always charge less than independent retailers selling the same products. There is no way a neighborhood hardware store can compete on price with the large national chains. Customers choose to shop at Bering's because of its fabulous merchandise assortment, the value of its services, great customer service, responsiveness to customer needs, and a consistently pleasant shopping experience. All this has earned it the reputation of "the Neiman Marcus of Hardware."

A LONG ROAD

August Bering and his brother, Conrad, opened Houston's first lumberyard, calling it A. Bering and Bro. They also operated a sash and door company together under the Bering Manufacturing Company name. The brothers eventually split; August took over the lumberyard and Conrad kept the manufacturing business. In 1940, August Bering Jr. founded Bering Lumber Company. After August Bering Jr. unexpectedly passed away, August Bering III took the reins. He relocated the lumberyard to the corner of Westheimer and Potomac, where it was destined to evolve into a remarkable retail business.

In those early days Houston's busy Westheimer Road was just two lanes surrounded by ranches and farmland. It wasn't long before the area was transformed into a premier shopping district housing many of the best-known upscale retailers in and around the world-famous Galleria Shopping Mall. Today the area bears no resemblance to the pastures that once prevailed. Bering Lumber thrived here for years, but by the mid-1960s the land where the lumberyard stood proved far too valuable to store lumber.

In 1968 the Berings converted what had been a lumber shed into a store and chose to concentrate on serving the needs of homeowners rather than selling lumber to builders. Timing was good: the nation's largest builders sought to buy directly from major lumber mills, a strategic change in the home construction business. About this time, August "Augie" Bering IV joined the business and now serves as chief executive officer, running the company along with chief operating officer Christopher Schmitz and Augie's children, Heather Bering and August Bering V.

Bering Lumber Company became Bering Home Center and the evolution began. The early 1970s saw the addition of a Gift Department and a large selection of household items such as pots, pans, and vacuum cleaners. The new concept grew and the future looked bright when, in the summer of 1971, tragedy struck—a fire entirely gutted the warehouse and all its contents. Although a devastating blow, the family rallied and chose to rebuild. With the help of a professional designer, they reconfigured the new store to reflect the changing merchandise selection and to better serve their customers.

A DIFFERENT KIND OF STORE

In June of 1979 Home Depot opened its first store and ultimately grew to be the largest home center chain in the country. Its dominance dramatically impacted local home centers and hardware stores throughout the nation. The Berings saw the expansion of Home Depot, Lowe's, and the like as an opportunity rather than a death knell. They knew that by creating a truly unique retail business, they wouldn't need to compete with national home center chains or other mass merchants.

Long before the folks at Starbucks thought to open its coffee shops in bookstores and supermarkets, Bering's installed a gourmet coffee bar in the store. Gourmet coffee proved so successful, it was logical that other gourmet products might be well received. The addition of chocolates, jellies, and a limited selection of packaged foods was a direct response to requests from customers in Bering's Westheimer neighborhood. Over the next few years Bering's expanded its housewares inventory, added gift baskets, and provided gift wrapping. These changes led the Berings into the bridal and baby gift registry business. After some time, this took off as well. While bridal registries were once exclusive to department stores, gift stores, and other retail establishments where traditional bridal gifts might be found, all that has changed in recent years. Today couples getting married are just as likely to want gifts from a store like Bering's as they are from a department store. For many couples a gift from Bering's may be even more desirable than traditional items found in a department store.

One product category Augie Bering sought was Baccarat crystal, but Baccarat was not about to sell its crystal to a store called Bering's Home Center, or any kind of hardware store for that matter. "When faced with this situation we invited the Baccarat folks to see our store," Augie recalls. "We also changed the name to just Bering's to reflect that we were far more than a home center." Bering's had become a very different kind of store, certainly atypical of a "home center" designation, so the name change was a logical next step.

With Baccarat's arrival at Bering's, other premium brands made their way into every department throughout the store. Housewares and home decor departments sell selections from Herend, Lalique, Waterford, and Spode, along with small appliances from Cuisinart and Viking. The Home Furnishings Department displays fine furniture, decorating accessories, and outdoor furniture, including outdoor kitchens with Fire Magic grills. The Children's Department, among the more out-of-the-ordinary categories for a hardware store, features baby clothing and toys, and the Stationery Department stocks Crane stationery and also notepads, custom bridal invitations, and a broad selection of upper-end pens, journals, and photo albums. Bering's carries a full line of Crocs-brand shoes for all ages, along with Jibbitz (those cute little decorations to put in the holes of Crocs). There's luggage plus backpacks, first-aid kits, desk accessories, wallets, bath and body fragrances, and pet supplies, including soap-on-a-rope for dogs.

Two other retailers chronicled in this book, Nell Hill's and Bronner's, excel at leveraging the holiday season. Christmas at this former lumber and home center rivals the best of them. Bering's makes a big deal out of the holiday season, transforming the store into a gift buyer's wonderland. In addition to a substantial selection of special gifts, Bering's adds classic decorating items to make any home festive for the holidays.

Even as Bering's adds product categories and new vendors, it maintains a stock of traditional hardware products for the convenience of its customers. Although traditional hardware amounts to less than half of Bering's inventory these days, customers can still find a washer to repair a faucet, a can of paint, or a specific tool for a do-it-yourself project.

A WILLINGNESS TO CHANGE

In some ways retailing as an industry can be slow and even reluctant to change, department stores being a prime example. Through the 1970s and 1980s, while such discount stores as Kmart and Wal-Mart opened across the country, department stores generally plugged along doing business as usual. They didn't see the threat nor did they recognize the opportunities enjoyed by lower-priced general merchandise stores with all the goods on one easy-to-negotiate floor. Rather than finding ways to differentiate themselves and offer more than the discounters, some actually cut back on specialty departments, making them little more than large apparel and shoe stores. Unfortunately, this is why so many have closed their doors or have been forced to merge. Consumers embraced large general merchandise discount stores as the next big thing in shopping convenience.

The Berings embrace change and do whatever they can to set their store apart from the competition. This culture allows the store and its staff to adapt to the needs of an ever-growing population of discerning residents in and around Houston's Westheimer neighborhood. In contrast to national home center chains that strive to position their stores as primary shopping destinations for a wide range of consumers, Bering's continually narrows and redefines its focus. This strategy ensures they properly attend to Houston's upscale community.

Bering's second store on Bissonnet in the West University Place district of Houston opened to meet the demand of their growing demographic. The merchandise selection varies between the stores, catering to the differing preferences of customers in each community. Some larger retail companies attempt to tailor their merchandise mix to a community but fall short if the buyers don't thoroughly understand customer wants and needs in each locale. At Bering's it is the way they do business.

DOES LISTENING TO CUSTOMERS REALLY WORK?

When I asked how Bering's evolved into the successful store it is today, Augie Bering IV looked me straight in the eye and said, "We listened to our customers and gave them what they wanted." About thirty years ago there was renewed interest in the concept of paying attention to customers to gain a better understanding of what they actually wanted. Over time, virtually every retailer in America affirmed that listening to customers was a great idea. Unfortunately, after much hullabaloo, decisions and priorities came about based first on cost considerations rather than customer considerations. Bering's never lets up. The customers' needs have been and always will be the driving force in this family's retail business.

Bering's e-commerce Web site was established by Heather Bering in 1999. Augie Bering V came on board in 2000 and is carrying the family business into the future. "My vision for Bering's future is to call out the special qualities that have made us successful in the past and make them into a promise. It then becomes our work and our choice to be who we say we are, and that is to exceed our customers' expectations, the Bering's way."

At a time when quality help in chain stores is but a memory of better times, the highly competent staff at Bering's enthusiastically advises customers on everything from complicated home repair projects to fixing a broken lamp. Hardware stores and home centers may appeal primarily to men, but the selection and breadth of merchandise available at Bering's makes it even more popular with women.

The question of whether a neighborhood store can survive and thrive amid the giants is answered by looking at Bering's in Houston. Generations of Berings built this terrific retail business by zigging while everyone else was zagging.

Bering's
6102 Westheimer Road
Houston, TX 77057
(713) 785-6400
www.berings.com

More photos of Bering's can be seen at
www.retailsuperstars.com/berings.

Wanna Buy a Watch?

Americans love to collect all kinds of stuff—some because it's rare, some because it's beautiful, some because it used to be someone else's, and some just because. They collect little things, like stamps, coins, and jewelry, and big things, like exotic automobiles. In Los Angeles Dr. Ken Jacobs, an avowed collector himself, built his business catering to the whims of those who collect watches. Ken's watch collection ranges from fine vintage timepieces to contemporary watches representing the best-known brands from Europe, Asia, and the United States.

HOW THIS CAME TO BE

Ken's early collecting began with seashells at age nine, shifted to stamps, and then to coins when he was given his grandfather's U.S. coin collection. Ken loved his coins, but after graduate school, in what seemed to him like a natural progression, his collecting interests turned to vintage pocket watches. In his quest for unique watches, he began attending flea markets and swap meets around Southern California, including the big one held at the Rose Bowl in Pasadena. It was there that he met and started doing business with a dealer who sold antique pocket watches at that monthly venue. This dealer generously mentored Ken and then referred him to other sources.

As his collection grew, Ken discovered he had an entrepreneurial bent—he enjoyed selling watches almost as much as he did buying them. At the time, he was a clinical psychologist working at a mental health facility. Recognizing a huge opportunity for a career change, Ken once again shifted focus, from pocket watches to quality wristwatches from the 1930s, '40s, and '50s made by such companies as Rolex, Patek Philippe, Omega, Hamilton, and Cartier. Wristwatches became his passion and he realized he would soon need a place where he could showcase and promote his collection.

In 1981, Ken rented a small space and set up shop within a friend's neon clock store located on Melrose Avenue. Melrose Avenue, beginning to gain popularity at that time, was destined to become among the best-known retail streets on the West Coast. Ken's timing couldn't have been better. The area boasted block after block of stores selling cutting-edge contemporary and vintage apparel, shoes, and jewelry. This hot new shopping district attracted large numbers of young shoppers as well as some of the entertainment industry's biggest stars, all looking for trendy fashion or just to take part in the Melrose scene. Many of these fashion-conscious shoppers found vintage watches to their liking. As Melrose Avenue gained popularity, another phenomenon was taking place all across the country and around the world—the popularity of vintage watches both as collectibles and as fashion accessories.

Ken let demand drive his growth strategy and kept his business expansion at a manageable pace. Once again opportunity knocked when Ken was invited to move into a larger nearby space in a vintage pottery shop called Slightly Crazed. During the mid-1980s, popular young actors Demi Moore, Emilio Estevez, and Judd Nelson strolled in, among the first of many movie stars to find Ken's watches irresistible.

Steady business growth allowed Ken to move into his first store exclusively for Wanna Buy a Watch? near some of Melrose Avenue's most popular retail destinations. He credits a great deal of his early success to the many young fashionable Japanese customers who came to Los Angeles to buy vintage American clothing, vintage collectibles, and, of course, vintage Rolex watches. If Rolex was not already the most popular brand at Wanna Buy a Watch?, it certainly came to be. Rolex was and continues to be the most popular and in-demand vintage watch brand in the world.

Wanna Buy a Watch? relocated again, this time to a much larger and grander Spanish-style building. Ken hired a designer who guided him in transforming the building into a beautiful 1920s mission-style watch and jewelry store. Wanna Buy a Watch? had now grown to 1,000 square feet. For the next ten-plus years the store sealed its reputation as "the" place in Southern California and the West to buy vintage and collectible watches.

Over the years, the eastern section of Melrose Avenue began to change and lost some of its luster, so in 2006 Ken once again relocated the store farther west on Melrose, closer to Beverly Hills. Today the store can be found in the more upscale neighborhood of Melrose Heights alongside some of Los Angeles's best-known home furnishings and apparel retailers. Stores from fashion designers Marc Jacobs, Carolina Herrera, and Diane von Furstenberg add to the allure of this highly desirable location with much better visibility and access, as well as ample and convenient customer parking.

VINTAGE WATCHES, MODERN CLASSICS, AND ANTIQUE DIAMOND RINGS

Although best known for its broad selection of vintage watches, Wanna Buy a Watch? also stocks hundreds of one-of-a-kind antique platinum diamond wedding rings, putting the store very much in the wedding ring business. Original Edwardian, art deco, retro, and modern designs from the early 1900s through the late 1940s make up this impressive collection. Some brides may be satisfied with a ring purchased at a mall that looks just like the kind all her friends have, but if she wants an antique ring that reflects the more elegantly detailed designs of an earlier era in jewelry, she can find it at Wanna Buy a Watch? The store sells not only vintage styles but also newly made gold and platinum earrings, bracelets, necklaces, and pendants inspired by the classic designs of the 1920s and '30s.

Owing to tremendous growth in the consumer marketplace, coupled with higher personal incomes in recent years, the value of collectibles and antique and vintage products of all kinds has increased significantly. Watches from such high-quality Swiss watchmakers as Rolex, Cartier, Omega, Patek Philippe, and Breitling certainly benefit from this run-up in value as well. In 2006, an extremely rare, 100-year-old watch from the German company A. Lange & Söhne sold at auction for $621,000. Among the most sought-after by vintage watch collectors is the Rolex Paul Newman Daytona. In 2007 and 2008, these watches were selling for $75,000 to $100,000. The market for rare and unusual watches from the most respected brands continues to command breathtaking prices from the collectors around the world.

The exclusiveness of owning and wearing a vintage watch from a prestigious company adds to the appeal. While rarity certainly brings about some of these high values, at least two other reasons account for the popularity of vintage watches. First, their beautiful designs reflect an elegance quite rare today. Second, the best vintage watches represent a level of craftsmanship not commonly seen in our world of mass-produced products. Anyone who enjoys beautiful design and fine craftsmanship, not to mention a nostalgic place in their heart, will appreciate the selection at Wanna Buy a Watch?

A TRULY MEMORABLE NAME

Branding a store name and making it part of our culture often takes years of advertising and hundreds or even thousands of stores. A good many independent stores sport clever names, but the phrase "Wanna buy a watch?" was part of American culture long before Ken named his store. It conjures up the image of that nefarious character in the trench coat sidling up to someone in the darkness. He opens his coat, revealing dozens of watches hanging from the lining, and pushes up his sleeves to show his arms covered up and down with watches. Amusing and memorable, the phrase paints a picture in the customer's mind and puts a smile on his or her face. It's an ingenious branding concept and certainly an excellent name for a store.

Ken now has more than twenty-five years' experience in the business, and his three key staff members have been with the store over ten years each. He employs only certified gemologists and highly skilled watch technicians to serve the store's customers. The clever name may get customer attention, but it also reflects the lighthearted personality of the store and the staff, which Ken believes is as much an ingredient to his success as fine products and expertise.

A store located on Melrose Avenue near Beverly Hills selling truly unique and collectible merchandise attracts the attention of movie and TV stars as well as famous musicians. The list of celebrities who frequent Wanna Buy a Watch? is extensive and has included stars such as Jennifer Aniston, Bono, Nicolas Cage, Sheryl Crow, Billy Crystal, Bruce Dern, Laura Dern, Danny DeVito, Mick Fleetwood, Jodie Foster, Anthony LaPaglia, Debi Mazar, Malcolm McDowell, Tom Petty, Brad Pitt, Ving Rhames, Carlos Santana, Mira Sorvino, and Denzel Washington. The store's Web site proudly posts an extensive list of the many stars who have shopped there in the last twenty-five-plus years.

"Over and over again, we hear our customers describe their experience shopping with us as 'personal,' 'attentive,' 'helpful,' 'informative,' and 'fun!' Selling is not always serious business at WBAW?, and may include a lot of playfulness and kibitzing." Ken further explains that his salespeople, being noncommissioned, makes it a noncompetitive, no-pressure retail environment. "Our salespeople's satisfaction (but not their paycheck) derives from completing a sale, providing good service, and matching the watch (or ring) to the customer." The obvious goal is for the customers to be thrilled with their purchases and "with the very personal and noncorporate experience of shopping with us."

BIGGER IS NOT NECESSARILY BETTER

Several of the retailers profiled in this book operate large, sprawling stores. Wanna Buy a Watch? beautifully presents its merchandise in a mere 1,250 square feet. With the exception of a lovely, antique oak dental cabinet situated behind the main counter and the oversize illuminated BIRT'S ROLEX store sign (the former namesake of a watch shop in London circa 1930), all the wood and glass display fixtures were custom built to provide a clean, classic, and rich look.

The store's Web site, wannabuyawatch.com, plays a crucial role in Ken's retail success. He uses the site to extend the store's reach to customers around the world. "As popular as our store is, as great as our location is," Ken remarks, "we could not survive on the revenues of the store alone if we had no Web site." The site features every single item in the store, individually photographed and described in detail. Customers are not expected to just "fill a shopping cart." Instead, Web visitors are encouraged to e-mail or call the store for assistance. That way, Ken and his staff can provide the same personal service they give to their face-to-face customers.

Local customers benefit from the Web site as well. Whenever new items arrive, they are immediately placed online. Customers can check the site regularly and see what's new. If they're interested in something, they can come in to see it in person. It's all about service, and by keeping the Web site current, Ken shows an understanding of and respect for the time constraints of his busy customers.

Selling one-of-a-kind items in an elegantly appointed store by extremely knowledgeable and friendly people makes up the formula for retail success. Other stores selling vintage watches exist, but I haven't found one other that combines such a captivating selection, friendly expertise, and first-class shopping experience as well as Wanna Buy a Watch?

WANNA BUY A WATCH?

8465 MELROSE AVENUE

LOS ANGELES, CA 90069

(323) 653-0467

WWW.WANNABUYAWATCH.COM

MORE PHOTOS OF WANNA BUY A WATCH? CAN BE SEEN AT WWW.RETAILSUPERSTARS.COM/WANNABUY.

Rowena's

When a visitor walks past the apron-clad, life-size mermaid and through the bright red door into the world of Rowena's, the sweet aroma of cakes baking in the oven gives a feeling of comfort and warmth, much like a big, welcoming hug. Frilly and fanciful with curly ribbons hanging from the ceiling, the gift shop decor complements the sweet treats sold within.

Rowena's makes every gourmet goodie by hand with tender loving care—from the jams, jellies, curds, and sauces to wonderful pound cakes and mixes. Each recipe is an original created by Rowena Fullinwider, the charming founder and namesake of this amazing business.

THE CAKE LADY

It all started with three fruit trees growing in Rowena's backyard. She gathered the crab apples, figs, and plums and transformed them into jams and jellies using her own creative genius. As the wife of a U.S. Navy officer, Rowena was often called upon by civic organizations in and around Norfolk to help raise funds for their various causes. To aid in these efforts, she baked almond pound cakes and put together holiday gift baskets. Her cakes were so popular, she became widely known as the "Cake Lady of Virginia."

Encouraged by steady, enthusiastic praise for her recipes and with an innate entrepreneurial spirit, Rowena soon ventured into the world of business. Like many visionary and hardworking entrepreneurs, she has enjoyed considerable success and recognition for her accomplishments and commitment to helping others achieve their own success.

THE BEGINNING

In 1983, with one employee, Rowena established her baking business in an old warehouse located within Norfolk's historic Ghent District, a small neighborhood near the city's commercial center. For several years, reluctant to give up her regular job, she ran the food company while continuing to work as a medical technologist in a local hospital. In 1989, she left the hospital and devoted all her time and energy to her growing gourmet food business.

One won't find automation at Rowena's. From the very beginning, unlike big food producers, the process of creating these wonderful treats was much like how Rowena prepared them from her home kitchen—in small batches—resulting in consistently high quality. The significance of this is that today Rowena's sells more than 80,000 cakes and 50,000 jars of jams, jellies, sauces, and curds every year— all made in small batches.

WHAT SMELLS SO GOOD?

Rowena and her capable staff cook up an incomparable selection of mouthwatering treats, including Carrot Jam (her most popular jam), Peach-Orange-Clove Jam, and Cranberry Nut Conserve; Luscious Lemon, Raspberry, and Key Lime Curds; Scrumptious Almond, Lemon, Key Lime, and Pecan Praline Cakes; Double Delicious Chocolate, Chocolate Mint, Chocolate Cappuccino, and Chocolate Turtle Cakes; Cranberry Lemon Tortes; and an enticing variety of little Tea Cakes.

Rowena's specialty treats qualify as works of art. She sculpts the Gift Package Cake, a heavenly almond pound cake, into a gift box with a huge cake ribbon around it made into a bow. Her cakes can be made in the shape of a rose, heart, star, or Easter egg. The artistry involved in making these handmade specialties is apparent in the detail of design, color, and, oh yes, taste.

THE GIFT SHOP AND TEA ROOM

Wait a minute! This is a book about stores and Rowena's does have a store—a very special store that attracts visitors from all over the eastern seaboard. At just a few hundred square feet, it is the smallest store in this book. But Rowena's gift shop is the place to try and buy the wonderful things made in the jam and jelly factory. In just three small rooms, visitors can purchase cookbooks, tea sets, and decorative plates, along with knives and spoons for serving the great-tasting items they have also bought.

Whether visitors come for a tour of the factory or a light lunch in the tea room, they almost always are drawn to the gift shop. Having visited Rowena's several times in recent years, it's always fun for me to spend time in the gift shop chatting with other visitors and whoever happens to be working in the shop that day, and, of course, tasting some of the great samples.

The beautifully decorated, authentic English tea room near the gift shop awaits hungry visitors. Intimate and elegant, the tea room seats fifty-four guests. An assortment of tea sandwiches, freshly baked scones, jams, cakes, curds, fresh fruit, salads, and a nice selection of teas make a visit to the tea room a delectable experience. Everything is served on lovely china and silver trays. Keeping in mind that children's tastes often differ from adults', Rowena's offers a special "Children's Tea." Choices for the Children's Tea include peanut butter and jam, grilled cheese, and turkey sandwiches; pretzel rods; carrots and dressing; and a variety of candies and cookies.

THE JAM AND JELLY FACTORY

Rowena's is far more than a gift shop and tea room. It is a thriving production facility, wholesale supplier, and mail-order gourmet food operation. The wholesale side of the business supplies Rowena's branded gourmet foods to several hundred retail stores nationwide, including A Southern Season, the excellent gourmet food store in Chapel Hill, North Carolina, also profiled in this book.

Catalogs mailed to consumers worldwide generate significant mail-order sales, especially during the holidays. More than 125 additional employees, hired to help the permanent staff of twenty, handle the increased holiday demand from Thanksgiving through the end of the year. Sometimes they temporarily close the tea room to put all their efforts into filling holiday orders.

Rowenas.com contributes significantly to the volume of sales originating outside the actual store. As the second Virginia food company to have an Internet site, Rowena's established its Web presence early on. In addition to being able to order all the beautifully photographed goodies made at Rowena's, the site provides additional information to visitors, including instructions on how to brew the perfect pot of tea. A photo posted on the site shows an army major stationed in Iraq enjoying a Rowena's cake. He writes, "Attached is a recent photo of me enjoying my lemon pound cake on the hood of my Humvee." He sliced the cake with his bayonet.

Visitors can tour the jam and jelly factory and watch the wonderful foods actually being made. It's a fascinating and fun experience for adults and children alike, and the aroma makes one's mouth water.

THE CAKE LADY'S ACCOMPLISHMENTS, AWARDS, AND HONORS

Building and sustaining a successful business requires discipline and hard work. Rowena Fullinwider not only enjoys business success but also devotes time to charities; small business associations; and community, state, and national women's organizations. She's served on the Chesapeake Bay Bridge and Tunnel Commission, Virginia's Small Business Advisory Board, and advisory boards of three local universities.

The U.S. Small Business Administration honored her with its Virginia Women's Business Advocate & Special Achievement Award, and the Virginia Retail Merchants Association named her Retailer of the Year. Rowena's has been featured in several lifestyle magazines, including *Southern Living, Redbook, Ladies' Home Journal, Bon Appetit,* and *Gourmet.* For all of Rowena's selfless accomplishments, former Virginia governor George Allen designated February 20, 1997, "Rowena Fullinwider Day."

Her most notable accomplishment involved taking on the Food and Drug Administration. In the Nutritional Labeling and Education Act of 1990, the FDA proposed requiring all producers of food, including small gourmet shops like Rowena's, to provide detailed nutritional labeling. The costs involved in doing the chemical analyses to comply would have been devastating to small businesses. She convinced the FDA to enact a small business exemption, which was subsequently passed by Congress. It is estimated that her persistence in this daunting battle saved as many as 9,000 small food processing businesses from closing their doors. Rowena was honored for her hard work by being elected in 1995 to President Clinton's Small Business Conference, where she co-chaired the Regulation and Paperwork Reduction Committee.

With so many companies fighting for customer attention, becoming a respected member of the community can only help a retailer bring attention to her business. Rowena has done that by getting involved with and giving back to the community in a wide variety of ways. She makes a great role model for other retailers, regardless of the size of their businesses.

ROWENA THE AUTHOR

As if she didn't have enough to keep her busy, Rowena added author to her list of attainments a few years ago. *The Adventures of Rowena & the Wonderful Jam and Jelly Factory* and *The Adventures of Rowena & Carrot Jam the Rabbit* are children's story cookbooks. The nine-year-old fictional Rowena featured in these stories bears a striking resemblance to Rowena's own daughter. For adults, there's the 270-page *Celebrate Virginia,* co-written by James Crutchfield and Winette Sparkman Jeffrey. This collection brings together 300 recipes from Virginia's kitchens, inns, and restaurants of yesteryear and includes 400 years of Virginia history laced throughout the book.

As I traveled the country researching this book, I met people who told me about special stores in their towns. I tried to visit as many of these stores as possible. When I arrived in Norfolk on other business, my host took me to Rowena's. I was quite impressed by the tea room, gift shop, and factory, but what really intrigued me was how Rowena had built her business. As we see every day, retailing can prove very challenging. The food business can be even more challenging, with literally thousands of companies—small, medium, and large—all vying for the attention of consumers, retailers, and distributors. In a business segment that requires nerves of steel and incredible determination, Rowena's thrives.

By every measure Rowena is successful and accomplished. Also a delightful hostess, she makes visitors feel truly welcome. For customers who can't get to Norfolk to shop in the gift shop or to taste her scrumptious treats in the tea room, the Web site is the next best thing.

ROWENA'S
758 WEST 22ND STREET
NORFOLK, VIRGINIA 23517
(757) 627-8699
WWW.ROWENAS.COM

MORE PHOTOS OF ROWENA'S CAN BE SEEN AT
WWW.RETAILSUPERSTARS.COM/ROWENAS.

The Silver Queen

Standing out in a sea of retail sameness becomes much less difficult when a store's narrow specialty compels several hundred customers from around the world to call on the phone, log on to its Web site, or visit the store every single day. The Silver Queen specializes in silver flatware, fine china, and crystal for the table, along with other kinds of silver merchandise and gifts. In creating such a highly focused business, the Arbutine family has made its store invaluable as a resource to hundreds of thousands of silver-seeking consumers.

FROM COINS TO FLATWARE

In 1972, after a career in the U.S. Air Force, Art Arbutine opened a 680-square-foot coin shop in the Tampa suburb of Belleair Bluffs, Florida. Along with buying and selling coins, Art and his wife, Pat, began buying and selling silver and gold jewelry, silver flatware, and other silver tabletop merchandise. Before long, the store grew from a simple coin shop into two distinct businesses. Having outgrown the original store long before moving into its new Largo location in 2002, the family managed to operate both businesses out of the one small space. Today Belleair Coins, Gold and Diamonds operates in a space next to The Silver Queen, both in a completely refurbished former bank building.

While the coin business continues to flourish, particularly at a time when the value of old coins, gold, and other precious metals surges, the breadth and depth of The Silver Queen retail business shows no limit to its growth potential. The exquisitely produced catalog, dynamic Web site showing thousands of products, and enchanting showroom/store, with its narrow merchandise focus and charming decor, attract customers from far and wide.

Americans generally live less formal lives today than in years past, but a good many households still enjoy the tradition of a more formal meal setting for holiday feasts, family gatherings, and entertaining friends. Chinaware, crystal stemware, and sterling flatware play an important role in that formality. Some younger Americans may show little interest in the more formal table settings, but those accustomed to using such traditional products value their importance and will carry on the practice for many years to come.

THE REPLACEMENT AND ADD-ON BUSINESS

It has been a long tradition for brides and grooms to register for gifts of flatware, along with other houseware items, when starting their new lives together. Over the last 100 years, the best-known flatware manufacturers and retailers have done an outstanding job selling complete sets of their wares to American households. The "for company" flatware has long been stored in elegant wooden boxes, to be used only on special occasions. That practice seems to be changing, with more and more people opting to use the "good silver" at everyday meals. On occasion knives, forks, spoons, or serving pieces get lost or damaged. If you've lost pieces because of garbage disposal mishaps or overenthusiastic dish scraping, you know how it feels when this occurs. That's when The Silver Queen comes to the rescue.

The store takes the replacement and add-on business very seriously. With its massive inventory of more than 12,000 patterns and 165,000 individual pieces, customer requests can usually be fulfilled immediately. Should a particular piece not be available, the customer will be placed on a waiting list and notified when the item comes in.

The Silver Queen actively buys estate merchandise from across the country. It then professionally restores all the estate pieces acquired and 100 percent guarantees its products to the customer's satisfaction. Approximately 75 percent of the flatware inventory comes from estate sales and 25 percent is new. The well-known sterling silver and silver plate manufacturers stocked at The Silver Queen represent such impressive brands as Baccarat, Christofle, Fabergé, Gorham, Oneida, Reed & Barton, Swarovski, Tiffany, Towle, and Wallace. Many exclusive patterns are available only from the Silver Queen. There is also a wide selection of chests in which customers can store their silverware; these come in dozens of styles and finishes.

The extent of the company's silver selection amazes customers, with merchandise for engagement and wedding gifts, births, and any special occasion one can imagine. Sterling silver letter openers, dinner bells, pillboxes, photo frames, water goblets, and tea sets, plus a wide array of sterling silver baby gifts, fill the store.

The Silver Queen, although best known for its tremendous selection of flatware and sterling silver merchandise, also offers crystal stemware and fine china from many of the world's most renowned manufacturers. The catalog presents a fine selection, but The Silver Queen's Web site makes available a comprehensive collection of both flatware and fine china organized by category, company, and pattern. Every item has been photographed, so even if a person doesn't know the exact pattern name, he or she can scour the inventory to find it.

A SPECTACULAR SHOWROOM

The Silver Queen's 4,500-square-foot showroom radiates elegance with its rich wood cabinetry custom built to best show the merchandise and fit the space. But the eight Waterford crystal chandeliers hanging from the tall ceiling give customers pause as they take it all in. These fabulous lighting fixtures enhance the merchandise presentation, making the store look even more spectacular.

In the showroom customers browse displays of china, crystal, and silver bowls; candlesticks made of china, crystal, and silver; a wide variety of decanters; glass and porcelain figurines; vases of all sizes and shapes; napkin rings; and clocks in a variety of materials and prices. There are even crystal bottle stoppers. A stunning collection of flatware, tea sets, and one-of-a-kind gifts, along with beautiful showings of Baccarat, Lalique, Orrefors, Royal Doulton, Waterford, and Wedgwood fine china and crystal, offer discerning shoppers infinite choices.

The store devotes a small area for the exhibition of quality antiques and select sterling silver pieces. These not-for-sale treasures, such as goblets, teapots, candelabras, and other precious silver pieces, are comparable to what one would expect to see in the hands of serious collectors or exhibited in museums.

TRUE EXPERTISE

In a world where expertise seems increasingly rare, cofounder Pat Arbutine and son Greg, the company's chief executive officer, rank among the nation's most respected experts when it comes to sterling and silver-plate flatware. Their "History of Silverware in America" presentation can be downloaded from The Silver Queen Web site. The Arbutines' expertise is tested daily when customers call inquiring about silverware styles, patterns, and brands. It's a rare day when Pat or Greg cannot answer a customer's question and provide insight and valuable information. What makes this expertise so remarkable is that some brands about which customers inquire have long gone out of business and their styles are either unavailable or available only through estate sales. But the Arbutines can still help them, illustrating just how far their expertise goes.

OWNING A NICHE

Several of the stores in this book serve narrowly defined consumer demographics. The Silver Queen not only appeals to a limited group of consumers, but does so with merchandise that in some cases has limited availability. Its massive selection of new and estate merchandise invariably meets the needs and expectations of this specific group of consumers.

While some retailers struggle as larger chains enter into narrower specialties, savvy independent merchants like Pat and Greg Arbutine recognize the opportunity and do what it takes to reach a broader audience. Adding a catalog and Web site to their tools for serving customers transformed The Silver Queen into a true multichannel retailer. Pat and Greg provide three clearly defined avenues for customers to acquire their merchandise. This multichannel approach levels the playing field for specialty retailers today. Retailing always will have a place for well-managed specialty stores with a clearly defined niche.

Greg Arbutine estimates that his core group of regular customers numbers 300,000. To satisfy these customers, The Silver Queen must stock just the right merchandise and provide every opportunity for customers to buy exactly what it is they want. The Silver Queen has carved its own niche and serves it well. In doing so, the Arbutines have enjoyed success and will undoubtedly continue to thrive for years to come.

THE SILVER QUEEN

1350 WEST BAY DRIVE

LARGO, FLORIDA 33770

(727) 581-6827

WWW.SILVERQUEEN.COM

MORE PHOTOS OF THE SILVER QUEEN CAN BE SEEN AT WWW.RETAILSUPERSTARS.COM/SILVERQUEEN.

Toy House & Baby Too

Consumers generally believe big-box stores like Toys"R"Us or mass merchants such as Wal-Mart and Target stock the largest selections of toys. While these giants undoubtedly prefer that consumers think this way, it turns out to be one of those retail myths perpetuated by marketing prominence.

Toy House & Baby Too of Jackson, Michigan, population 36,000, stocks the largest selection of toys and baby products in the United States—more than any single Wal-Mart, Target, or Toys"R"Us. It's more common for independent toy retailers to sell an assortment of educational merchandise out of small, boutique-type stores. A few other independents around the country do carry a larger selection of toys than the big guys. Johnny's Toys in Covington, Kentucky, just outside Cincinnati, Ohio, stocks a selection of approximately 22,000 toys, and Kazoo & Company in Denver, Colorado, averages 16,000. By comparison, Wal-Mart, Target, and other general merchandise retailers stock a limited selection. Typically the largest Toys"R"Us stores carry up to 16,000 toys and the smaller ones as few as 9,000. An average Wal-Mart or Target stocks approximately 4,500 toys. This number increases for the Christmas season.

Toy House & Baby Too stocks a whopping 32,000 toys from more than 550 manufacturers. While certainly not the largest in physical size or even total sales, it is the nation's largest toy store when considering selection. And consumers love choices, especially when it comes to toys for their kids.

Phil Wrzesinski, owner of Toy House & Baby Too, and his team of buyers carefully select toys for the store based on value, educational merit, and inherent ability to engage and delight children. Mass merchants prefer toys with large-quantity sales potential and those that fit into a particular price point. In the national chain stores, shoppers most likely will find a good selection of toys and games supported by tie-ins with television shows and hit movies or those supported by national advertising campaigns. By contrast, Phil looks for toys that encourage creativity and imagination, involve the child in play, or can hold the child's interest for weeks, months, or even years. This approach to buying and selling toys has allowed this independent store to grow and prosper for over sixty years.

IT REALLY WAS A TOY HOUSE

After serving his country in World War II, Phil Conley, Phil Wrzesinski's grandfather, was determined to find a fun career in which people were happy all the time. For a while he worked for a fire truck manufacturer, selling fire trucks to various municipalities. Not being satisfied with the work, he took a job with the phone company. Neither of these efforts proved particularly enjoyable. He and his wife, Esther, knew that a place filled with toys would put smiles on people's faces and it would certainly be fun selling toys. Jackson, Michigan, didn't have a specialty toy store at the time and, except during the Christmas holidays, people had to drive to Hudson's Department Store in Detroit, an hour away, to buy toys. So in 1949, Phil and Esther bought an old house in Jackson, and Toy House came to be.

Another retailer opened a baby store around that time and ultimately failed, so Phil and Esther bought the inventory and incorporated it into their toy store. As it turned out, toys and baby goods complemented each other and made a good fit in the store. Today the store's name reflects both merchandise categories—Toy House & Baby Too.

As the business grew, the Conleys expanded the original house several times but eventually outgrew the space altogether. In 1967, they moved into a larger space in order to offer more toys that they knew their customers would love.

Phil Conley became very involved in the community, serving as city commissioner and chairman of the planning commission. After being elected mayor of Jackson, he left the day-to-day operations of the business. Eventually Phil and Esther sold the business to their son-in-law, Chuck Wrzesinski, and daughter, Sue. Chuck and Sue's son, Phil Wrzesinski, represents the third generation heading up this family business.

The entire family follows the standard of serving the community set by founder Phil Conley's service in city government. Sue was a longtime board member of the Jackson Community Foundation, Jackson's main philanthropic organization. Chuck served for years on the Midtown Association and was responsible for all the downtown Christmas decorations through the 1980s. Phil Wrzesinski currently serves as president of the Midtown Association, sits on the board of the Jackson Retail Success Academy, and is a founding member of the Jackson Local First Independent Business Alliance. "Giving back to the community is one of the values Phil Conley inspired in all of us," Phil says with pride.

A TREMENDOUS SELECTION

While the sheer number of toys and baby merchandise impresses shoppers coming into the store, the breadth of merchandise amazes them as well. The Toy Department includes action figures, games, puzzles, wooden trains, stuffed animals, and blocks from LEGO, Playskool, Mattel, and Gund. The Activity/Crafts Department offers beads, lanyards, Play-Doh, crayons, paints, and supplies for school projects from Crayola, Melissa & Doug, and Bead Bazaar. The Science Department carries telescopes, microscopes, bug catchers, dinosaurs, and magnets from Educational Insights, Wild Planet, Orion, and Smithsonian.

The Sports/Outdoors Department displays wagons, bikes and trikes, sandboxes, and sporting equipment from Razor, Step2, and Radio Flyer. The Hobby Department has rockets, electric trains, models, and airbrushes from Tyco, Lionel, and Atlas. The Baby Department displays cribs, bedding, car seats, strollers, swings, and high chairs from Britax, Crown Crafts, and Best Chairs. Toy House serves the scouting community as an authorized area dealer for both Boy and Girl Scouts of America. It's unlikely that a customer won't find what he or she wants.

The Toy House & Baby Too building measures 30,000 square feet, with 16,000 square feet devoted to the showroom and 14,000 square feet reserved for the warehouse and offices. As a bonus to an already wonderful shopping experience, a large parking lot sits directly in front of the store for shopping convenience, a luxury a good many downtown retailers don't enjoy these days unless they own the property.

A CHALLENGING BUSINESS

In recent years some of the largest toy retailers have struggled to survive. For a long time Toys"R"Us ranked as the largest company in the business, with the greatest number of stores and highest sales volume. That was before Wal-Mart entered the scene. Wal-Mart tends to dominate a category once it decides to take it on. With thousands of stores, Wal-Mart quickly became the nation's dominant toy retailer by expanding its selection and lowering prices on the most popular toys. This proved to be a difficult time for Toys"R"Us. No longer a publicly held company, Toys"R"Us is now owned by a private investment firm and it has begun to refocus and reinvent its business.

KB Toys, with most of its stores located in shopping malls, is another national toy chain experiencing great difficulties. KB's high-rent locations have negatively affected its ability to compete directly with Wal-Mart and other discounters. The company declared bankruptcy in 2004. Shrinking from nearly 1,000 stores to fewer than 400, KB emerged from bankruptcy in 2005 and continued to close stores. As this is written, the company is liquidating the remaining stores.

Toy House & Baby Too, an independent, single-store retailer, is able to survive and thrive in this environment because it focuses its merchandise selection on toys that help children learn and enjoy their playing experiences. The people working in the store develop strong relationships with customers while providing a higher level of customer service than can be found in a big-box or mass merchant's store. They encourage customers to browse for as long as they want. Being in the store makes people happy; it's a fun place for families to spend time.

MORE THAN JUST SELLING STUFF

In addition to his fabulous selection of merchandise, Phil Wrezsinski offers several services not available from others in the business of selling toys. The well-trained staff assembles bikes, wagons, baby cribs, strollers, outdoor toys, and other "needs assembly" items. The store delivers to customers in Jackson County and nearby communities, provides free gift wrapping, runs a gift registry for baby showers and the like, and promotes a teacher loaner program, lending educational toys to teachers for use in the classroom. Toy House & Baby Too makes free layaway available to its customers, a service not so common in these days of multiple credit cards.

Buying and properly installing a car seat ranks right up there with the most difficult and important challenges new parents face. The Toy House staff amiably helps parents install car seats, even if they were purchased elsewhere. The store also offers prospective and new parents invaluable learning opportunities. A series of classes titled "Shopping for Baby 101" provides insights into how to buy high chairs and baby room furniture, as well as car seats and strollers. Instructors demonstrate how certain baby products are used and the differences between them. Rather than using these classes to pitch the store, they have been designed specifically and solely to educate and inform.

Phil publishes an e-mail newsletter overflowing with information about new toys as well as "how to's" for buying toys and baby merchandise. His "Top Ten Toys," a guide to the best toys ever created, can be downloaded from the store's Web site. Back issues of the newsletter and lots of other information can be found on the Web site as well. "While other stores seem to offer less and less service," Phil explains, "we are attempting to raise the standards for ourselves to heights we have not previously reached in terms of education, helpfulness, and just plain having fun."

A SIGNIFICANT BUSINESS FOR A SMALL TOWN

In smaller communities such as Jackson, many retailers struggle to attract customers. Yet Toy House & Baby Too draws customers from all across southern Michigan and is able to bring those customers back again and again. That's no small feat in a marketplace with such national chain competitors as Wal-Mart, Kmart, warehouse retailer Meijer, and two Toys"R"Us locations.

Rather than focus its marketing efforts solely on the 163,000 people in the immediate metropolitan area, the store's advertising is broad based to reach prospective customers throughout southern Michigan. The marketing plan places a major emphasis on radio but uses some television and direct mail as well. In a geographic area not far from larger cities like Lansing, Ann Arbor, and Detroit, radio very effectively promotes this destination store.

When I interviewed Phil, he explained part of his unusual marketing strategy. "We bring the customer into the store by advertising the baby department. While they are in the store we work on building a relationship with the customer with the goal of selling toys to them through the child's growing-up years." The result? Toy House & Baby Too attracts parents whose children are still quite young. The baby they are shopping for today will one day need gifts for his or her first birthday, then for the second and the third. That same baby may one day need Girl Scout or Boy Scout paraphernalia. All of these things can be purchased at Toy House & Baby Too throughout the child's growing-up years.

With a large percentage of the store's customers coming back year after year, it is not unusual for multiple generations of a family to do business with the store. A good many customers who grow up in Jackson and then move away stay loyal to Toy House & Baby Too; they buy toys for their children and grandchildren as they grow.

Although neighborhood toy stores may be dwindling, this one competes quite well in spite of the national chains. When Toys"R"Us first opened nearby, some people thought it might be the demise of

Toy House. In fact, the opposite occurred—business increased. After some customers were drawn to the location by the new Toys"R"Us, they came back to or visited Toy House & Baby Too. More often than not, they fell in love with Toy House & Baby Too or renewed their relationship with this marvelous independent store. Everything there is better—the selection, the service, the people who know what they're talking about and so obviously enjoy what they're doing, and the long relationships the customers cherish with the Conley and Wrzesinski families and friendly staff.

Toy House & Baby Too has a mission: "We're here to make you smile!" Everything about this store does just that.

TOY HOUSE & BABY TOO

400 N. MECHANIC STREET

JACKSON, MICHIGAN 49201

(517) 787-4500

WWW.TOYHOUSEONLINE.COM

MORE PHOTOS OF TOY HOUSE & BABY TOO CAN BE SEEN AT

WWW.RETAILSUPERSTARS.COM/TOYHOUSE.

Hartville Hardware

An estimated 25,000 hardware stores and home centers exist in the United States. This includes such large chains as Home Depot, Lowe's, and Menards, as well as co-operative buying groups like Ace Hardware, True Value, Do it Best, and Hardware Hank. The three largest retail chains operate nearly 5,000 stores, so it's easy to see how difficult it can be for a single-store retailer to stand out and thrive in a highly competitive category.

To combat the buying advantages of the large national and regional chains, independent hardware stores band together by joining cooperative buying groups. The cooperative buys collectively and uses its leverage to create and disseminate its marketing message. Annual and semiannual trade shows bring the individual retailers together to network and to attend educational programs. Even with the power of the cooperative behind them, independent hardware stores and home centers face real challenges and their numbers continue to dwindle year after year.

Rather than trying to compete on the same level as the big guys, independent hardware retailers find that their best chance for survival is to serve local consumers in small towns and rural communities situated a good distance from large cities. But serving small local populations limits their potential for significant sales volume. That is, unless they take steps to differentiate their stores and make them desirable destinations for consumers from distant communities. And so we begin the story of Hartville Hardware, owned and operated by brothers Howard and Wayne Miller since the early 1970s.

A QUICK HISTORY

Over the years the small town of Hartville supported several hardware and farm store businesses. In 1972, Howard Miller bought a 5,000-square-foot hardware store and brought in his nineteen-year-old son, Howard Jr., to manage it. The newly married Howard Jr. got a crash course in the hardware business from the former owner and proved to be a quick study. His brother, Wayne, helped out after school, and they were on their way. It only took two years to outgrow that 5,000-square-foot store, and in August of 1974 the brothers broke ground on a 22,500-square-foot building situated on four acres of land.

By the end of the year, the new Hartville True Value opened for business. Howard Jr. never dreamed they would need more than 22,500 square feet; it seemed so huge at the time. But it proved way too small for this thriving enterprise, and over the years several additions were built. In 1987, a 6,000-square-foot section was constructed to add a John Deere department; since opening, it has become a leading John Deere dealership in Ohio. By 2002, the brothers decided to end their relationship with TruServ, the parent company of True Value, and go with Do it Best, another hardware buying cooperative. Hartville True Value became Hartville Hardware. Today, the business covers more than 100,000 square feet at this location. Another building about a mile away houses the catalog and Internet business. The challenge for the future will be how to continue to grow the store now that they've run out of land.

A TRUE FAMILY BUSINESS

The Miller family business ventures started long before Hartville Hardware. Back in the late 1930s, Sol Miller, Howard Sr.'s father, bought a piece of land and started the Hartville Livestock Auction. When Sol died in 1958, Howard took over the livestock auction. Howard later opened a gas station and grocery store, which later became a dry goods store. In 1966, Howard closed the dry goods store and opened a restaurant that seated seventy-five, including the serving counter. The restaurant proved to be popular from the start, selling all meals for $1.00, except shrimp, which went for $1.25. While no longer selling meals in the family restaurant for $1.00, they still live by the philosophy of giving customers great value. This is fundamental to the way the Millers do business.

Eventually Howard closed the livestock auction and converted the gas station into a coin shop. As time went on, Howard's sons, sons-in-law, and other family members joined in and took the helms of the various businesses. They all maintain the same ethical approach and high business standards instilled in Howard by his father, Sol.

TOOLS, TOOLS, AND MORE TOOLS

Hartville Hardware does a perfectly good job selling merchandise to the people in its immediate community—fewer than 2,500 people live in Hartville—but with such a small population, the business can't rely solely on local sales to generate sufficient dollar volumes. Fortunately, Akron, Youngstown, Canton, and Cleveland are all within an hour's drive. Unfortunately, several Home Depots, Lowe's, and other hardware stores lie within easy driving distances as well. So why would a customer choose to shop at Hartville Hardware?

The answer is very simple—tools. Hartville Hardware specializes in tools. It is one of the biggest and best tool merchants in the nation. It carries every kind of tool imaginable, in every size, quality level, and price point available. From the common to the extremely rare, Hartville Hardware, and its online tool division, is the resource to which craftspeople of all kinds turn.

That's not to say that Hartville Hardware doesn't carry other hardware products. It ranks among the best independent hardware stores anywhere in the country, selling everything from John Deere tractors and building materials to home decorating items and boxes of nails. It's what a community hardware store should be, with a wide selection and core commitment to serving customers.

Howard and Wayne Miller knew that if they were to survive, they needed to be different and special. The first step the brothers took toward establishing their business as a dominant tool retailer was to buy truckloads of power tools. With such high-quantity buying, they could negotiate excellent prices with the suppliers. The second step was to offer substantial discounts to consumers. In the early days this price advantage helped establish the store as Ohio's largest retailer of tools. When Lowe's and Home Depot began opening stores in the area, the price advantage became less of a factor. To continue building the tool business and maintain their position in the marketplace, a new strategy became necessary.

By broadening their selection and adding woodworking tools, they filled a need for consumers and accomplished their goal. Hartville

Tool Woodworking mailed its first catalog in the early 1990s. Its emphasis on woodworking tools, particularly hard-to-find tools, solidified Hartville Hardware's reputation with buyers across the country. The catalog and Internet business that is Hartville Tool Woodworking continues to grow and now occupies its own building. The 160-plus-page full-color catalog and extensive, easy-to-navigate Web site sell everything one needs for any woodworking project—from saws, drills, jigs, chisels, hammers, and mallets to specialized marking and measuring devices, cabinets and workbenches, finishing products, and how-to books and DVDs.

THE SEMIANNUAL TOOL SALE

Hartville Hardware's highly anticipated tool sale takes place in November and February. Over the years the tool sale has grown into one of the largest events of its kind anywhere in the United States. The bigger of the two sales, held the second weekend in November, draws thousands of customers. While customers regularly drive from more than an hour away to shop in the store, the tool sale attracts customers from neighboring states as well. The draw is so great that parking presents a bit of a challenge. For this event, determined customers park anywhere they can, some as far as a mile away from the store.

In addition to the great tool prices offered during the sale, the store serves up free refreshments, and representatives from the top manufacturing companies explain how to use their products. The selection of both power and woodworking tools is massive. One recent Hartville Hardware tool sale resulted in more than 12,000 transactions, amounting to over $1 million in total sales.

MORE THAN TOOLS, TOO

Located not far from the hardware store sit the other Miller family businesses. The sprawling Hartville MarketPlace occupies what originally was the livestock auction venue. This unusual marketplace, open four days a week, consists of 110 individually owned shops— selling everything from fresh meat to T-shirts to home furnishings— as well as an outdoor, twenty-acre flea market with several hundred more vendors selling their wares.

In front of Hartville MarketPlace sits the 100,000-square-foot Hartville Kitchen, one of the highest-volume restaurants in Ohio. This current incarnation of Howard Sr.'s little restaurant that opened in 1966 feeds stick-to-your-ribs country-style lunches and dinners to customers from all around the Midwest. In addition to its large dining room, which seats 440, and banquet facilities, which accommodate up to 500, the building houses Hartville Collectibles, a sizable gift and collectibles shop; a bakery and candy shop where Hartville Kitchen's delicious homemade pies and salad dressings can be purchased; an art gallery; and Hartville Coin & Jewelry. The Miller family businesses together offer diverse shopping choices for area visitors.

ALWAYS THE PEOPLE

Throughout the research for this book I looked for keys to the long-term success of these retailers. Did they have anything in common? One constant I found was the quality of the people hired to work in the stores. The great retailers profiled in this book understand friendly, knowledgeable people to be a key ingredient in building a successful retail business that will last for years. Hartville Hardware's extremely knowledgeable staff ably guides customers into making informed selections for the tools and hardware they may need for any particular job. The value of highly knowledgeable, helpful people cannot be overstated.

When a retailer abandons that strategy, as is the case with Home Depot, sales suffer. Home Depot started out employing skilled carpenters, painters, plumbers, and electricians to work in its stores. They served their customers well and the company grew into the largest home center retailer in the country. When management changed and a take-no-prisoners, cost-cutting approach was adopted, most of those full-time craftsmen got caught in the cross fire. Without skilled employees, Home Depot's sales suffered and its sterling customer service reputation was tarnished.

As single-store retailers, Howard and Wayne Miller understand the folly of such a strategy change. They were able to build a successful hardware business—even though surrounded by fierce competition—because of two basics. One, they offer a selection of tools and other merchandise unavailable elsewhere. Two, they hire friendly, attentive, and highly knowledgeable people to work in the store. This combination of assets serves as Hartville Hardware's survival guide, as it does for many of the stores chronicled herein.

Several specialty stores claim legions of customers and "fans" who just like to visit certain kinds of stores. Electronics stores, computer stores, and shoe stores come to mind, and, yes, hardware store fanatics exist as well. For anyone who grew up in a town with a great hardware store, a visit to Hartville Hardware will spark wonderful memories. The store is chock-full of every kind of item you would expect in a great hardware store and much, much more. In today's retail marketplace, with so many stores that fail to deliver on any kind of meaningful promise, Hartville Hardware raises the bar to Olympic levels.

HARTVILLE HARDWARE

940 WEST MAPLE STREET

HARTVILLE, OHIO 44632

(330) 877-3631

WWW.HARTVILLEHARDWARE.COM

MORE PHOTOS OF HARTVILLE HARDWARE CAN BE SEEN AT

WWW.RETAILSUPERSTARS.COM/HARTVILLE.

A Virtual Tour of the Stores

One of the great things about today's technology is that I can tell the story of these wonderful retailers in more than just words. You can take a virtual tour of the twenty-five stores and see with your own eyes more of what makes them so successful. We have built a Web site showing interior photos of the stores so you can see how the use of architecture, store design, merchandising, and special features make these stores unique and why customers enjoy shopping in them so much.

You will see Jungle Jim's full-size fire truck on top of the hot sauce display, Gallery Furniture's giant television screen in the front showroom, Rowena's beautiful English tea room, the stuffed animals on every level of Estes Ark, the golf-related art gallery at In Celebration of Golf, hundreds of Christmas lights at Bronner's Christmas Wonderland, the giant high-heeled shoe staircase at Junkman's Daughter, and so much more.

So I invite you to visit the Web site and take a tour of these extraordinary stores at www.retailsuperstars.com.

Are There More Retail Superstars?

If you own or know of other successful, independent, one-of-a-kind stores, I am very interested in hearing about them. Whether I write another book or feature them on our Web site, I will continue looking for and telling the stories of America's Retail Superstars. Please either send an e-mail to info@whalinonretail.com or call me, toll-free, at 800-766-1908.

Stores in Alphabetical Order by Name

Stores in Alphabetical Order by State

Acknowledgments

....

Retail Superstars would not exist without the help of many people.

The motivation for this book initially came from conversations I had with retail reporters. They often asked whether I thought Wal-Mart and other national chains were going to put independent and smaller chain retailers out of business. Weak ones, I would say, but then I'd tell them about the many independent stores that continue to grow and prosper regardless of the competition. So, thank you, reporters, for giving me the idea to tell the story of twenty-five of the many successful independent retailers thriving in America.

I also want to thank my literary agent, John Talbot. When I set out to look for an agent to represent this book, my goal was to find someone who was as excited as I was about telling the story of these amazing stores. After my first conversation with John, I knew he was the agent I wanted to represent me and this book. When John set out to find a publisher, the goal of finding enthusiasm was the same. Thank you to Jeffrey Krames at Portfolio for his confidence in me and enthusiasm for the book; to Jeffrey's right hand, the equally enthusiastic Jillian Gray; to the marketing team, Allison McLean and Christine D'Agostini; and to all the other people at Portfolio who helped get the book published. What a wonderful team!

Everywhere I go in my travels, I visit stores, not only to keep a handle on the retail climate but also in the hope that maybe, just maybe, I'll discover a store that can be called remarkable. Spending time getting to know the retailers profiled in this book was a privilege and a pleasure. I found them all to be dynamic, interesting, passionate people. In every case they enhanced my knowledge and understanding of the retail business and how to prosper in today's competitive environment. The nation's business press and consumer media do a great job of profiling the largest chains and interviewing their leaders. But by limiting themselves to the big guys, they miss out on meeting some of America's most interesting business leaders or entrepreneurs and finding out about their stores.

The extraordinary merchants and stores profiled in this book are: Michael Barefoot of A Southern Season, Paulette Cole of ABC Carpet & Home, Bob and Michael Abt of Abt Electronics, Mark Pahlow of Archie McPhee, Augie Bering of Bering's, Wayne Bronner of Bronner's Christmas Wonderland, Susan and Steve Swickard of Estes Ark, Jim McIngvale of Gallery Furniture, Marta Benson of Gump's, Howard and Wayne Miller of Hartville Hardware, Roger and Kathy Maxwell of In Celebration of Golf, Jim Bonaminio of Jungle Jim's International Market, Pam Majors of Junkman's Daughter, Mark Gavron of Junkman's Daughter's Brother, Debi Greenberg of LouisBoston, Mary Carol Garrity of Nell Hill's, Michael Powell of Powell's City of Books, Ed Moriarity of Ron Jon Surf Shop, Rowena Fullinwider of Rowena's, Pat and Greg Arbutine of The Silver Queen, Kevin Pipes of Smoky Mountain Knife Works, Sue and Phil Wrzesinski of Toy House & Baby Too, Ken Jacobs of Wanna Buy a Watch?, Wilkes Bashford of Wilkes Bashford, and Saul Zabar of Zabar's. I am grateful to all of them for the opportunity to tell their stories.

The original idea for this book and the stores profiled herein came from me. Any mistakes you might find are all mine. The task of editing and clarifying my thoughts and words has fallen into the highly capable hands of Terri Pilot, the best partner anyone could have. This is the second book on which we have collaborated, and the results are just as satisfying. She simply is the best!

I spent twenty-five years as a retailer before starting Retail Management Consultants in 1987. As a voracious reader, I've learned a great deal about retailing and retailers from the hundreds of books I've read on the subject. I have also had the opportunity to learn from the many retailers I've worked with as a consultant and speaker over the years. Now I can add the tremendous experience of writing this book. Any time I work with or interview a retailer, I learn. So much of successful retailing depends on creativity, daring, and hard work. This has taken a lifetime and there's so much more to learn.

About George Whalin

George Whalin's experience in retail is extensive and firsthand. He started his career on the sales floor and worked his way up. In the 1960s, he opened and managed the original Guitar Center on Sunset Boulevard in Hollywood, California. He sold instruments to the Beatles, the Rolling Stones, the Jackson Five, the Grateful Dead, and many more well-known and not-so-well-known musicians. After leaving the musical instrument business, he became the senior training manager for a 125-store consumer electronics chain.

In 1987, George founded Retail Management Consultants. The company provides business-building services to retail and consumer products companies all across North America. He has consulted with a wide range of organizations in every area of retailing, from single-store merchants to leading national chains. As one of the nation's most highly respected retail experts, George is regularly quoted in *USA Today*, the *Wall Street Journal, BusinessWeek, U.S. News & World Report, CNNMoney*, and numerous trade magazines and newspapers across the country. He's a regular guest on radio and TV newscasts commenting on current retail and consumer issues.

George is a highly sought-after speaker, each year delivering dynamic speeches and information-packed seminars for retail companies, associations, and consumer products manufacturers and suppliers across North America and internationally.

For information on how to put George Whalin to work for your organization, call (800) 766-1908; locally and outside the United States call (760) 431-2910. You can reach George via e-mail at info@whalinon retail.com or write to Retail Management Consultants, 2382 Camino Vida Roble, Suite L, Carlsbad, California 92011-1508.

About Retail Management Consultants

Retail Management Consultants, founded by George Whalin in 1987, provides services for retail organizations as well as consumer products manufacturers. With a focus on increasing sales and maximizing profits, services provided to retail organizations include:

+ Strategic planning
+ Operational evaluation
+ Improving workforce performance through training and education
+ Development of in-store merchandising programs
+ Creation of business-building marketing programs

Services provided to consumer products manufacturers and wholesalers include:

+ Customized sales and product training programs for retail salespeople
+ Improvement of in-store positioning and merchandising of products

For more information, contact:

RETAIL MANAGEMENT CONSULTANTS
2382 CAMINO VIDA ROBLE, SUITE L
CARLSBAD, CA 92011-1508
(800) 766-1908 OR (760) 431-2910
E-MAIL: INFO@WHALINONRETAIL.COM
WEB SITE: HTTP://WWW.WHALINONRETAIL.COM